Disney
THE LION KING

MUSIC FROM THE MOTION PICTURE SOUNDTRACK

T0070970

ISBN 978-1-5400-6560-5

Visit Hal Leonard Online at
www.halleonard.com

Contact us:
Hal Leonard
7777 West Bluemound Road
Milwaukee, WI 53213
Email: info@halleonard.com

In Europe, contact:
Hal Leonard Europe Limited
42 Wigmore Street
Marylebone, London, W1U 2RN
Email: info@halleonardeurope.com

In Australia, contact:
Hal Leonard Australia Pty. Ltd.
4 Lentara Court
Cheltenham, Victoria, 3192 Australia
Email: info@halleonard.com.au

CONTENTS

CIRCLE OF LIFE/NANTS' INGONYAMA

Moderately, with an African beat
NANTS' INGONYAMA
Music and Lyrics by LEBOHANG MORAKE and HANS ZIMMER

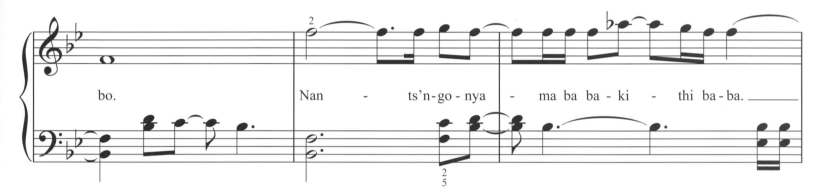

Same tempo, gently rhythmic

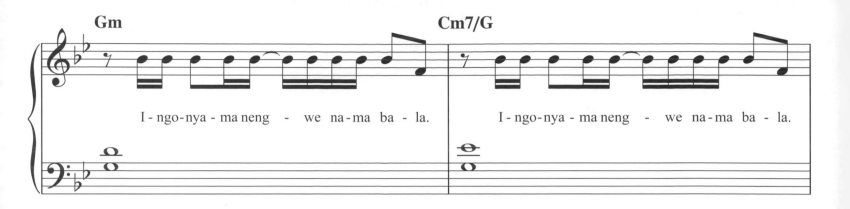

Gm

I - ngo-nya - ma neng - we na-ma ba - la.

Cm7/G

I - ngo-nya - ma neng - we na-ma ba - la.

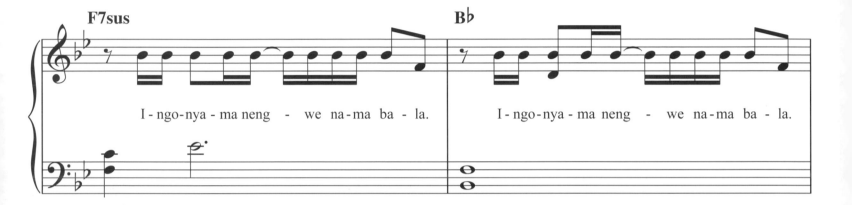

F7sus

I - ngo-nya - ma neng - we na-ma ba - la.

B♭

I - ngo-nya - ma neng - we na-ma ba - la.

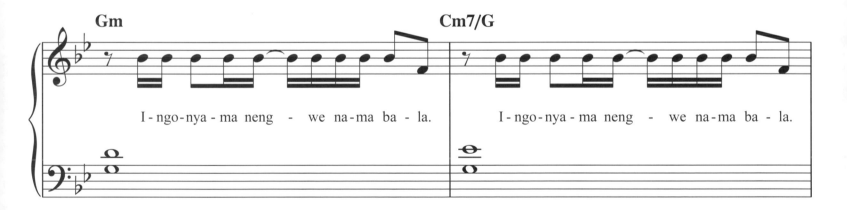

Gm

I - ngo-nya - ma neng - we na-ma ba - la.

Cm7/G

I - ngo-nya - ma neng - we na-ma ba - la.

CIRCLE OF LIFE
Music by ELTON JOHN
Lyrics by TIM RICE

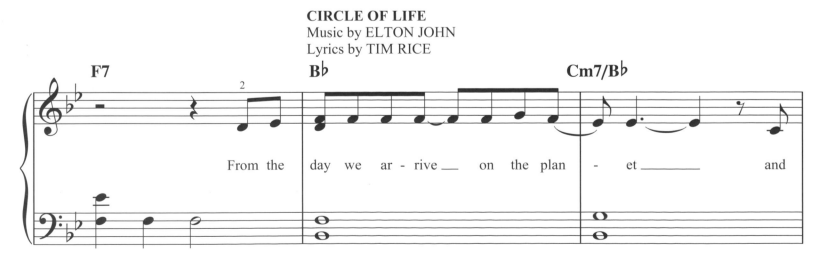

F7

B♭

Cm7/B♭

From the day we ar-rive ___ on the plan - et _____ and

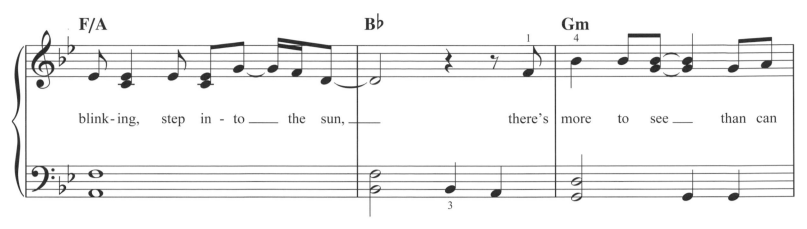

blink-ing, step in - to ___ the sun, ___ there's more to see ___ than can

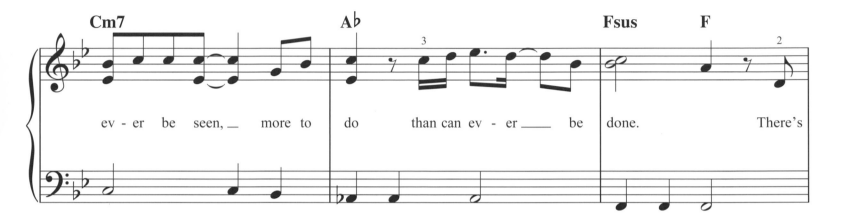

ev - er be seen, ___ more to do than can ev - er ___ be done. There's

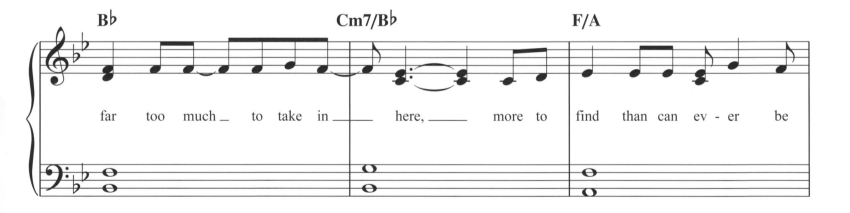

far too much ___ to take in ___ here, ___ more to find than can ev - er be

found. But the sun roll-ing high ___ through the sap-phi-re sky ___ keeps great and

small on the end - less round. It's the cir - cle of life,

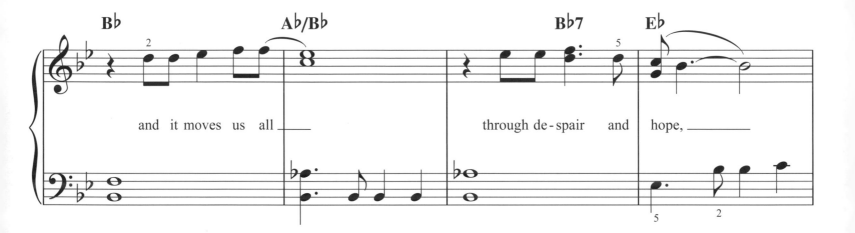

and it moves us all through de - spair and hope,

through faith and love, 'til we find our

place on the path un - wind - ing

in the cir - cle, _____ the cir - cle _____

of life.   *mp*

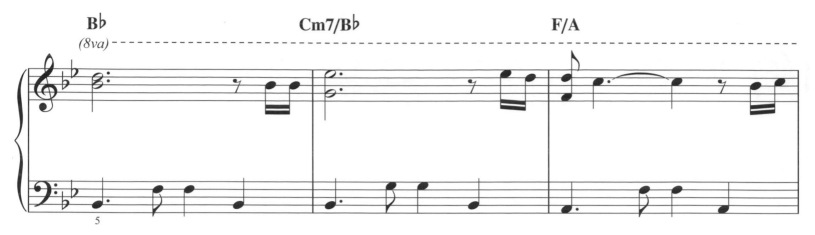

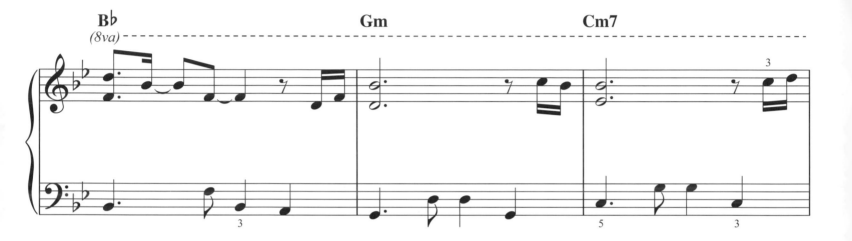

It's the cir - cle ___ of life,

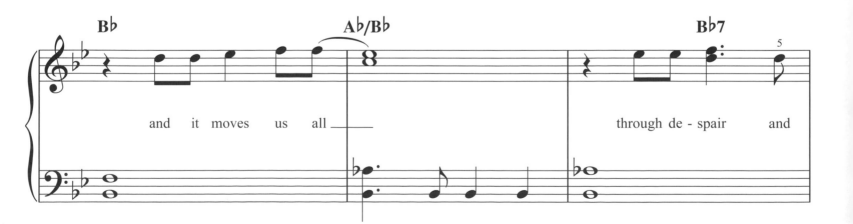

and it moves us all ___

through de - spair and

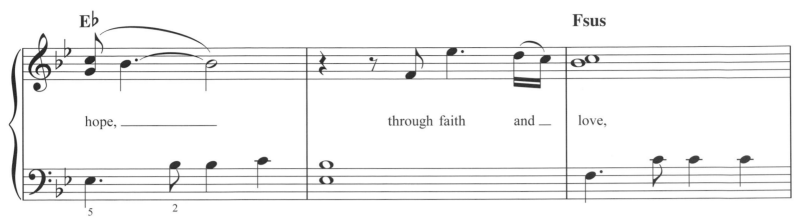

hope, _____ through faith and _ love,

'til we find our place _____ on the path un -

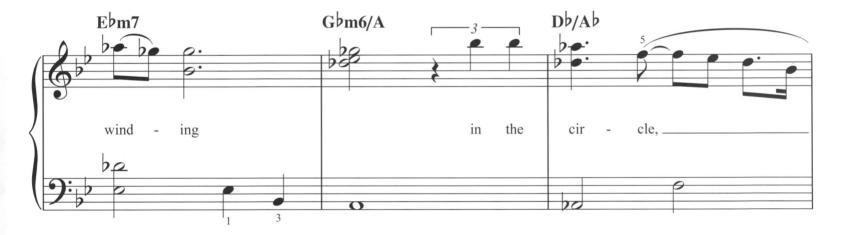

wind - ing in the cir - cle, _____

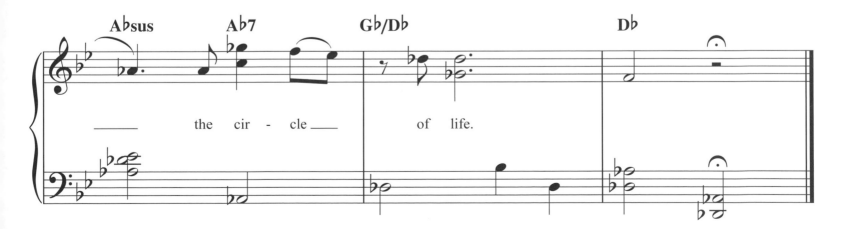

_____ the cir - cle _____ of life.

RAFIKI'S FIREFLIES

Composed by
HANS ZIMMER

Slowly, in 2

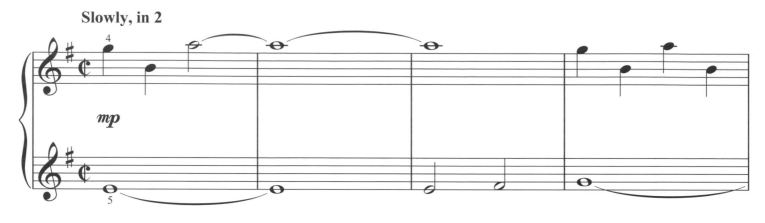

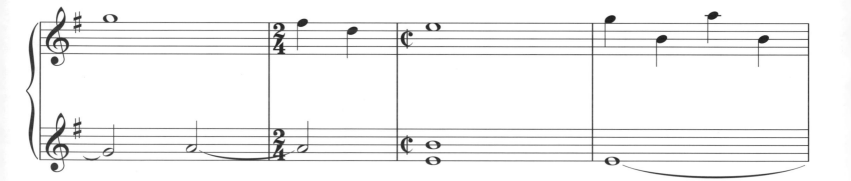

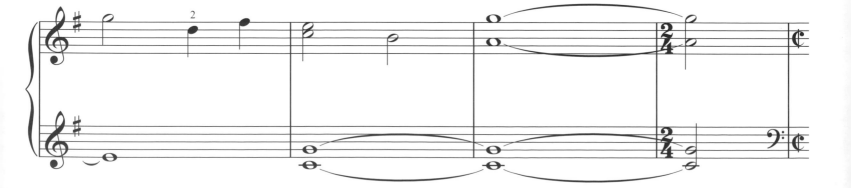

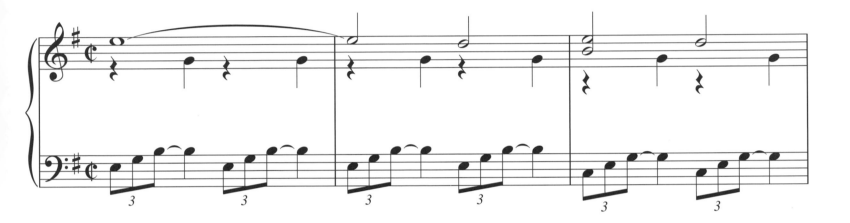

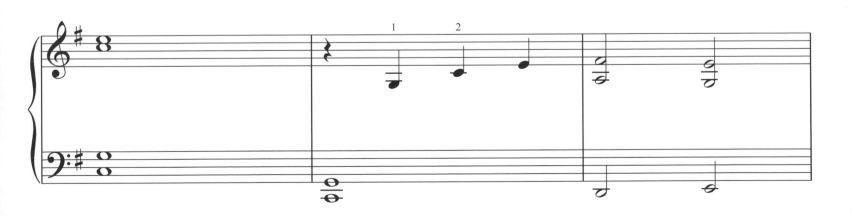

Slightly faster

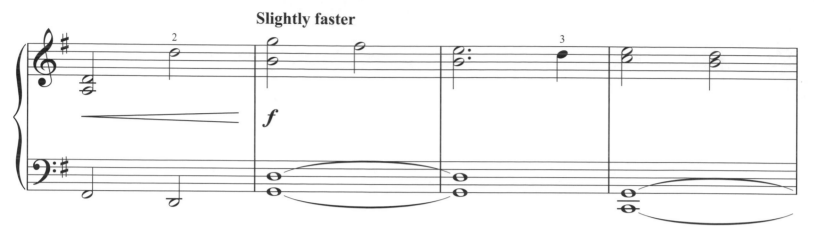

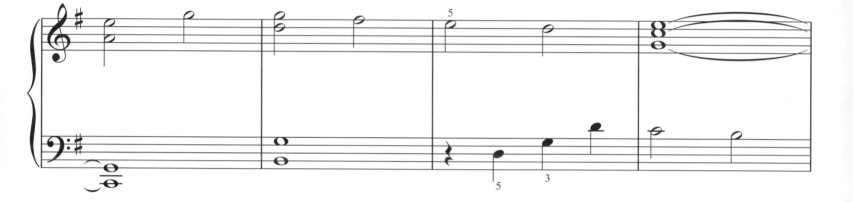

I JUST CAN'T WAIT TO BE KING

Music by ELTON JOHN
Lyrics by TIM RICE

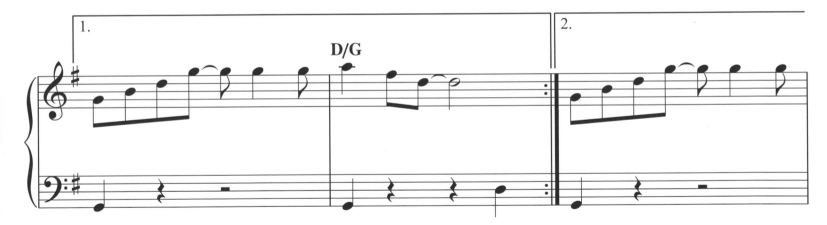

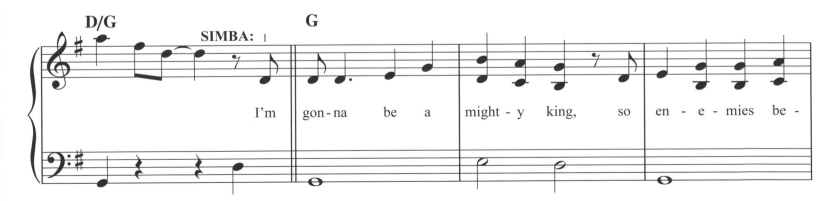

SIMBA: I'm gon-na be a might-y king, so en-e-mies be-

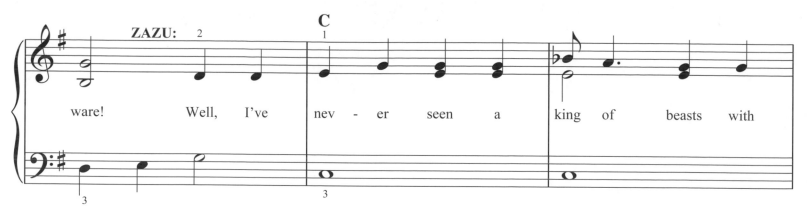

ware! Well, I've nev - er seen a king of beasts with

quite so lit - tle hair. I'm gon - na be the mane e - vent, like

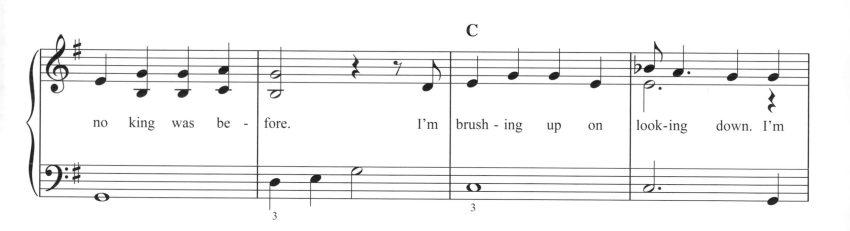

no king was be - fore. I'm brush - ing up on look - ing down. I'm

work - ing on my roar! Thus far, a rath - er un - in - spir - ing

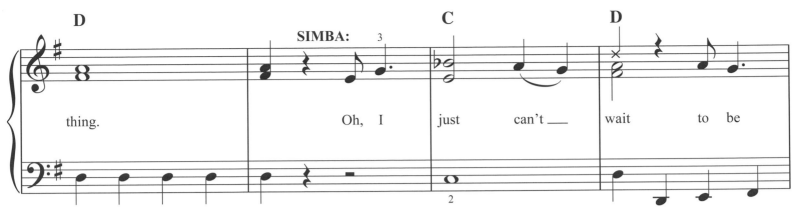

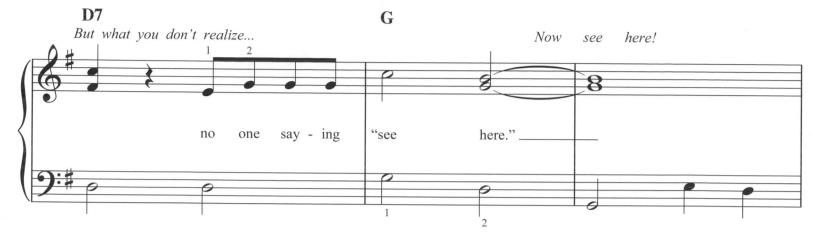

D7

But what you don't realize...

G

Now see here!

no one say - ing "see here." _____

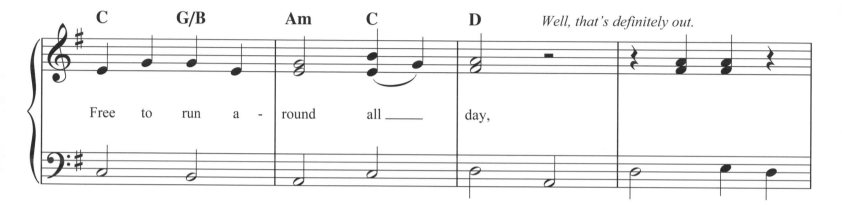

C **G/B** **Am** **C** **D**

Well, that's definitely out.

Free to run a - round all _____ day,

C **D** **G**

free to do it all my _____ way!

ZAZU:

(Quasi spoken) I think it's time that you and I ar -

ranged a heart - to - heart. *(Sung)* Kings don't need ad - vice from lit - tle

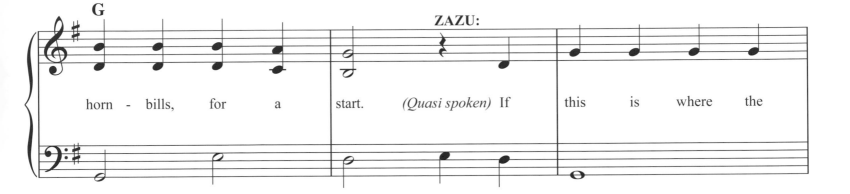

horn - bills, for a start. *(Quasi spoken)* If this is where the

mon - ar - chy is head-ed, count me out! Out of ser - vice, out of

Af - ri - ca. ___ I would - n't hang a - bout. *(Sung:)* This child is get - ting

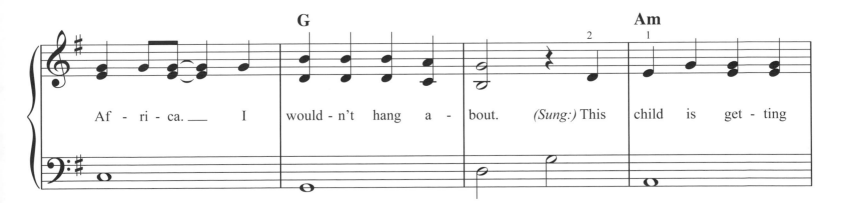

D   **SIMBA:**   **C**

wild - ly out of wing!   Oh, I just can't ___

D   **G**

wait   to be   king!

C

F/C   **C**   **G/C**

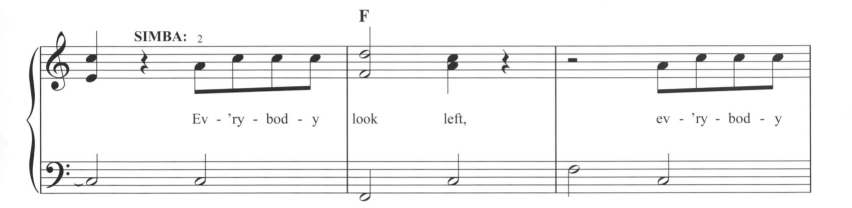

Ev - 'ry - bod - y look left, ev - 'ry - bod - y

look right. Ev - 'ry - where you look, I'm

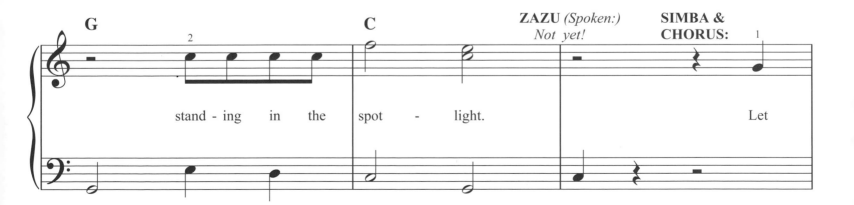

stand - ing in the spot - light. Let

ZAZU *(Spoken:)* *Not yet!*

SIMBA & CHORUS:

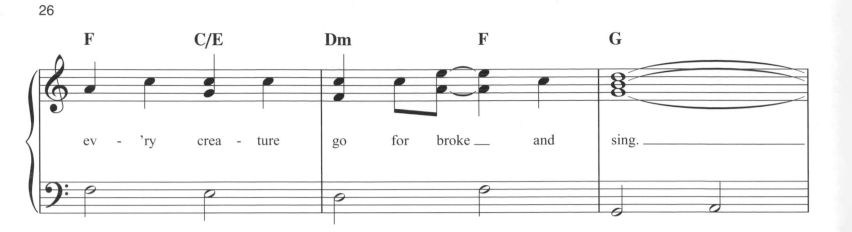

ev - 'ry   crea - ture   go   for   broke ___ and   sing. _____

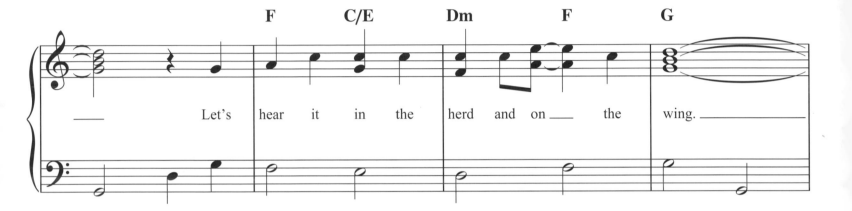

___   Let's   hear   it   in   the   herd   and   on ___ the   wing. _____

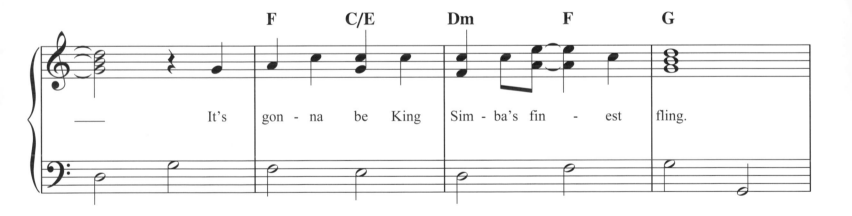

___   It's   gon - na   be   King   Sim - ba's   fin - est   fling.

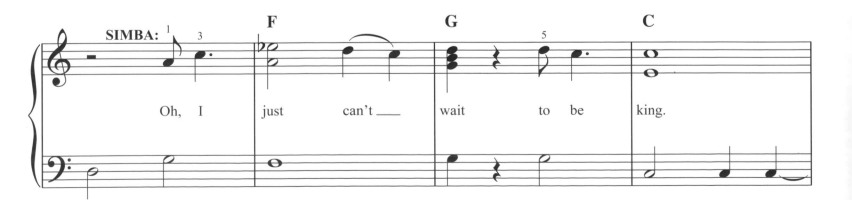

SIMBA:

Oh,   I   just   can't ___ wait   to   be   king.

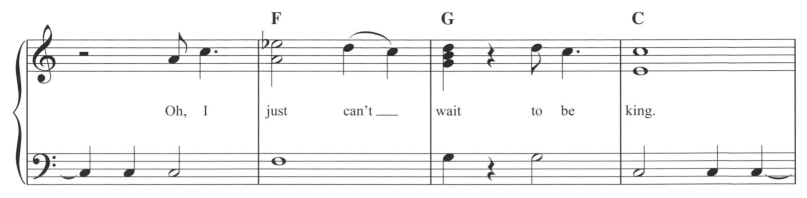

Oh, I just can't ___ wait to be king.

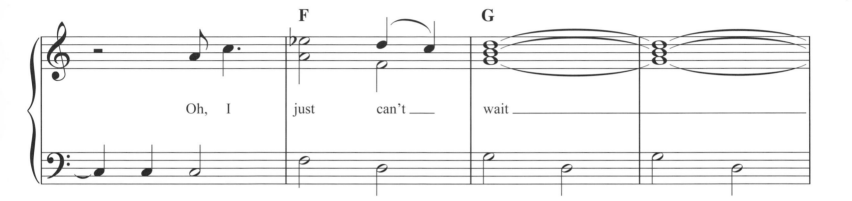

Oh, I just can't ___ wait ___

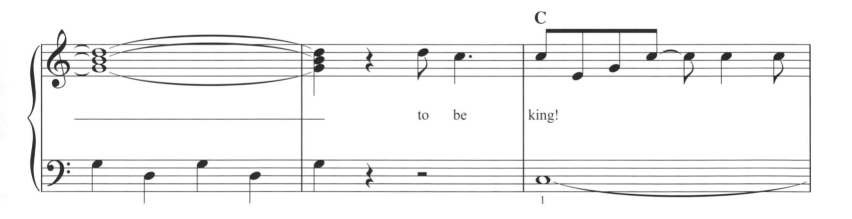

___ to be king!

BE PREPARED
(2019)

Music by ELTON JOHN
Lyrics by TIM RICE

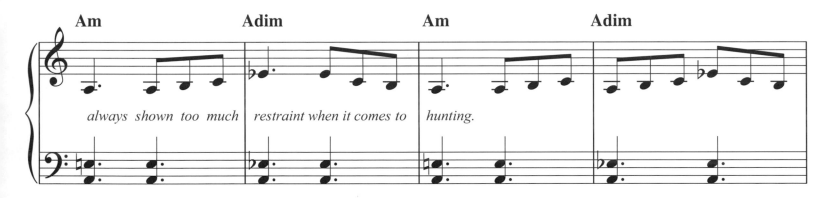

Am SHENZI: **Adim** SCAR:

Mufasa is far too *powerful to challenge.* Mu-

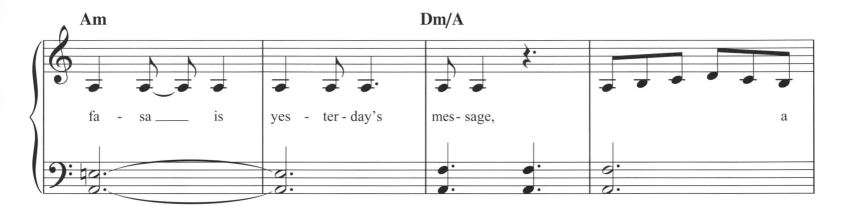

Am **Dm/A**

fa - sa____ is yes - ter - day's mes - sage, a

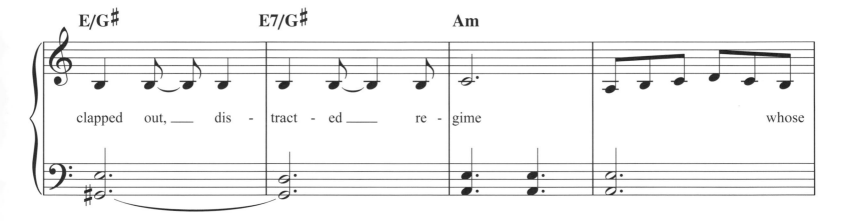

E/G♯ **E7/G♯** **Am**

clapped out,___ dis - tract - ed___ re - gime whose

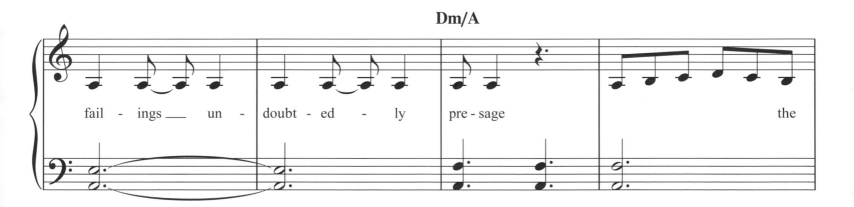

Dm/A

fail - ings___ un - doubt - ed - ly pre - sage the

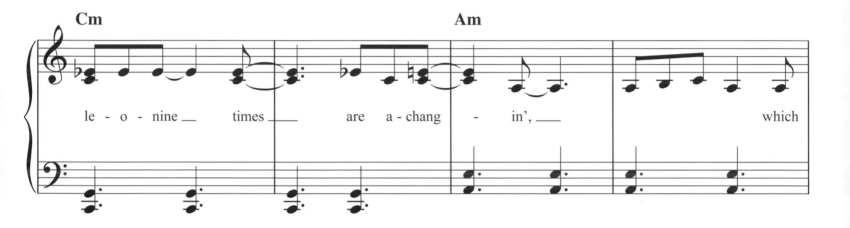

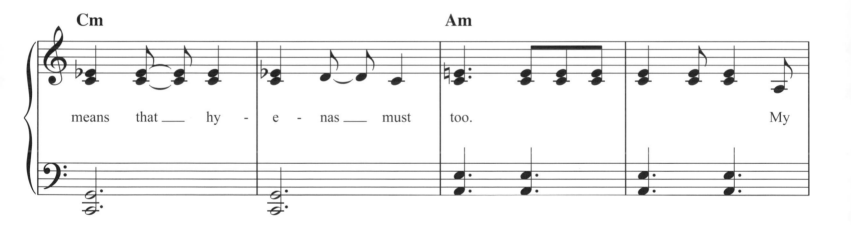

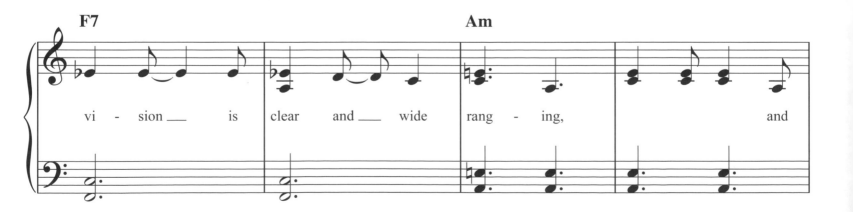

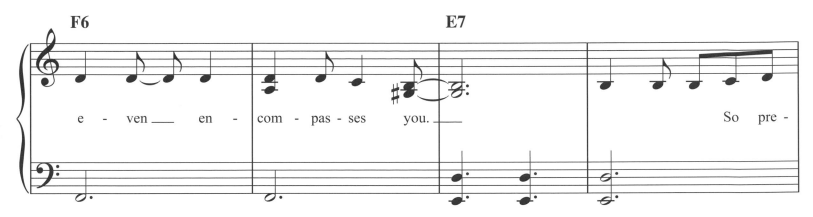

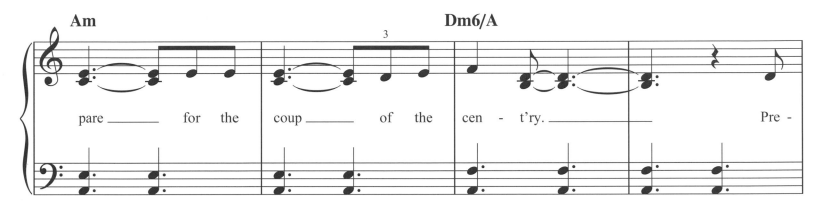

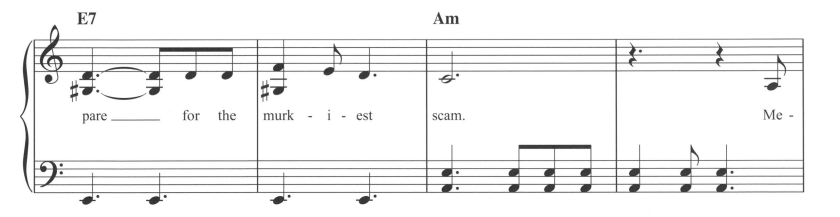

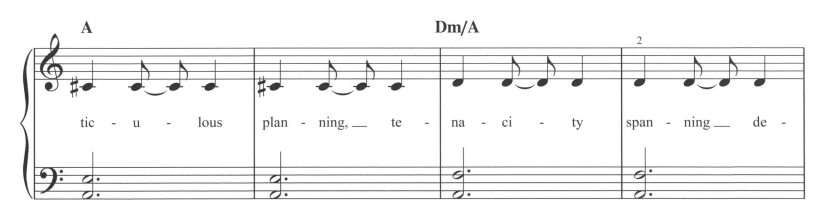

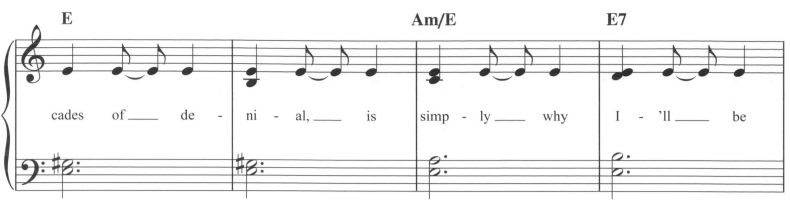

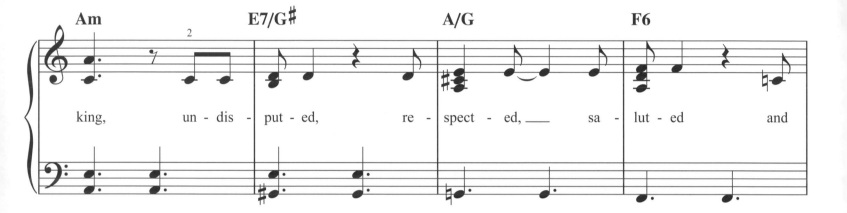

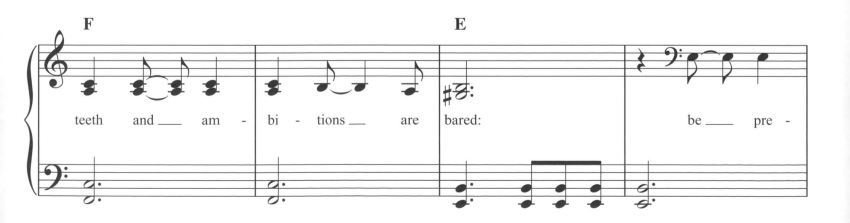

Am

HYENAS:

pared. _____

Be pre -

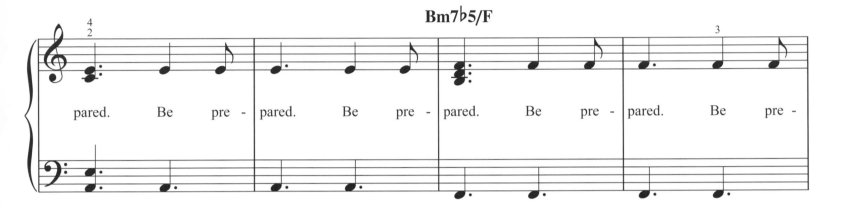

Bm7♭5/F

pared. Be pre - pared. Be pre - pared. Be pre - pared. Be pre -

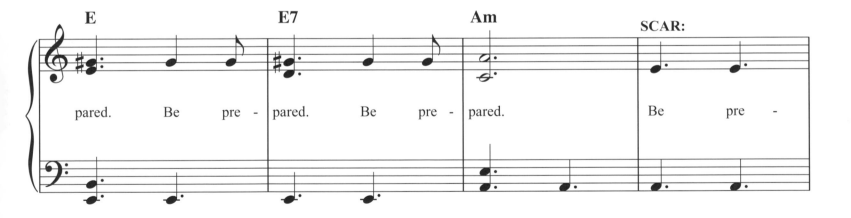

E   E7   Am

SCAR:

pared. Be pre - pared. Be pre - pared.   Be pre -

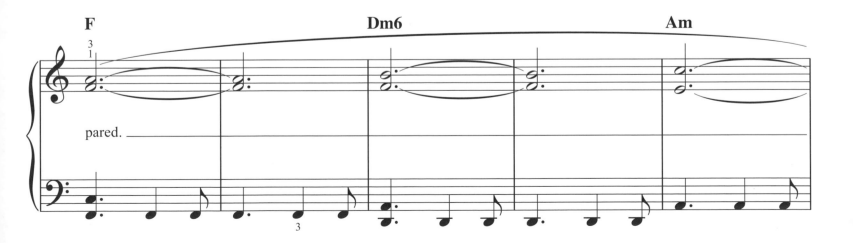

F   Dm6   Am

pared. _____

34

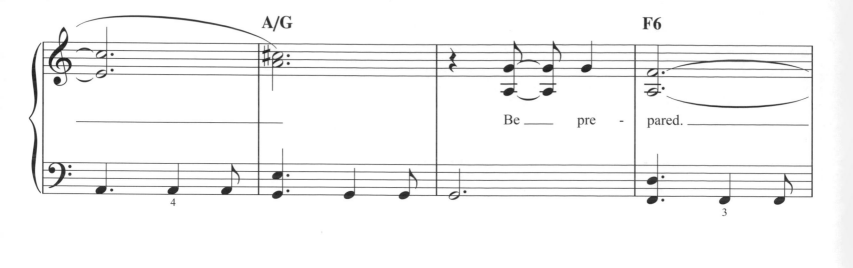

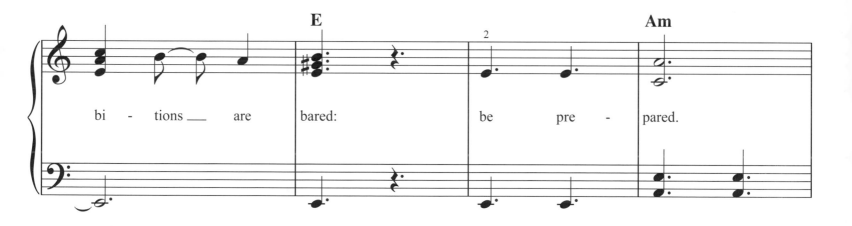

SCAR TAKES THE THRONE

Composed by
HANS ZIMMER

Moderately slow

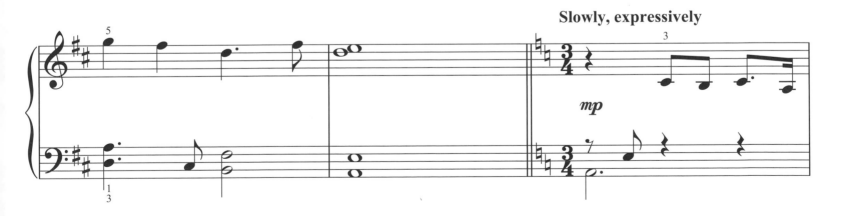

Slowly, expressively

STAMPEDE

Composed by
HANS ZIMMER

Moderately, in 1

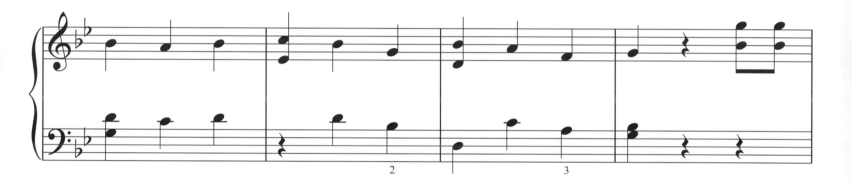

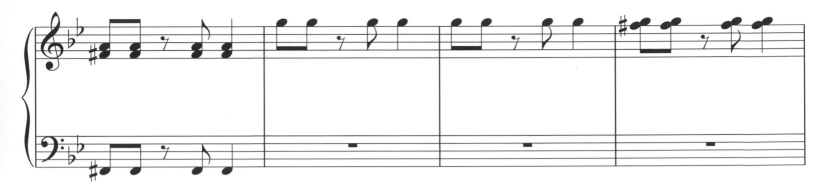

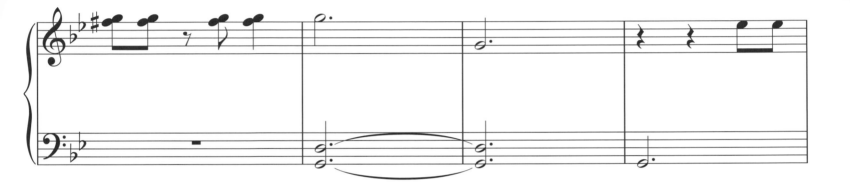

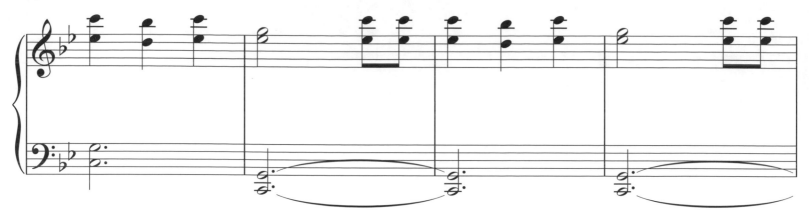

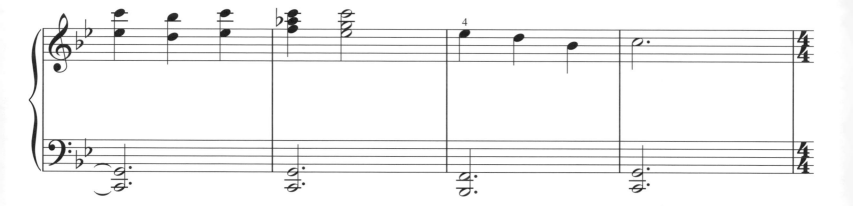

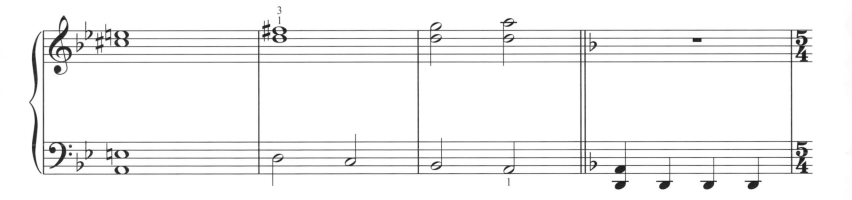

43

Quickly, in 2

mf

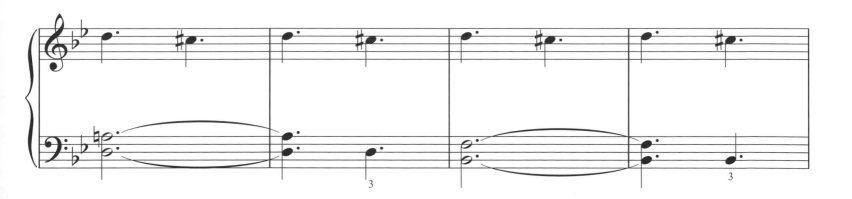

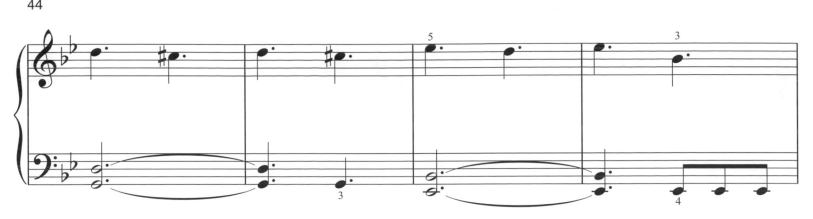

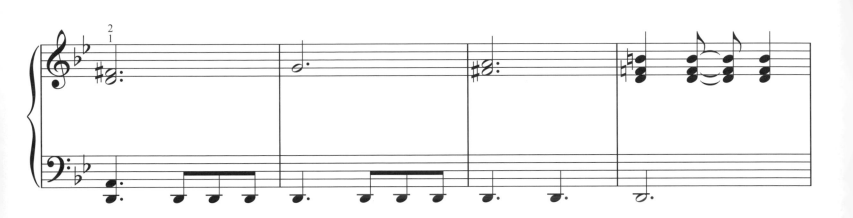

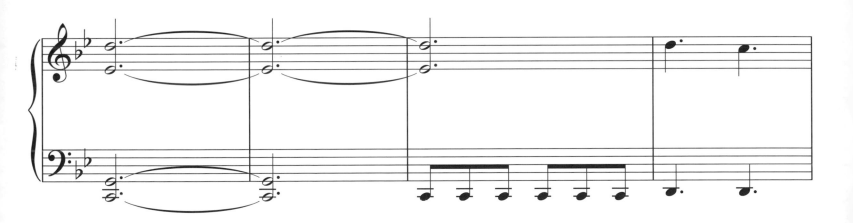

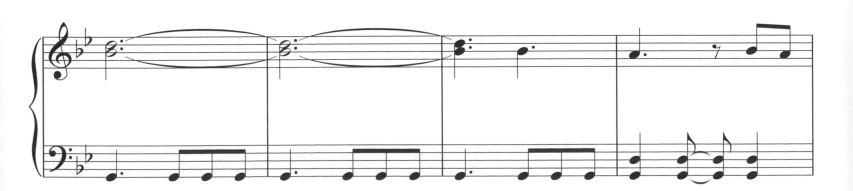

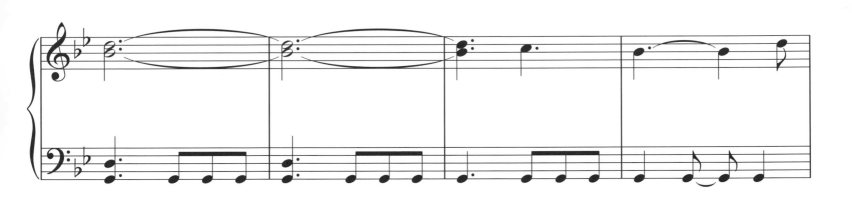

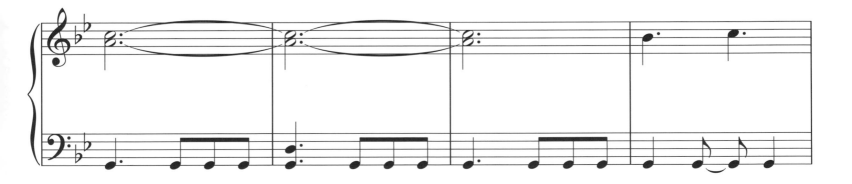

Half as fast

HAKUNA MATATA

Music by ELTON JOHN
Lyrics by TIM RICE

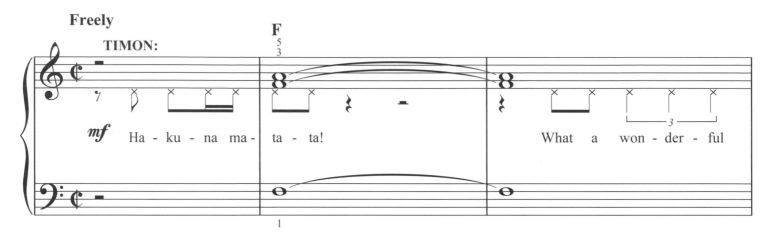

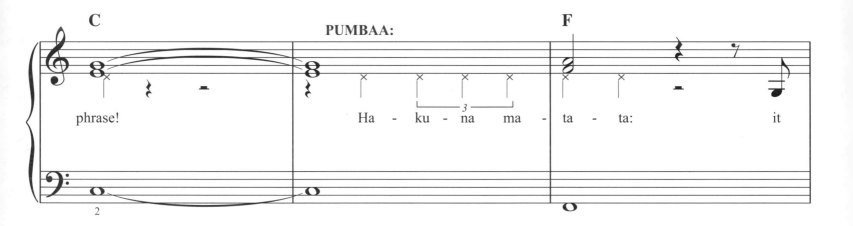

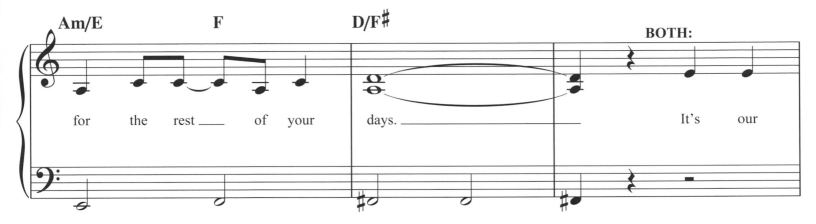

for the rest _____ of your days. _____ **BOTH:** It's our

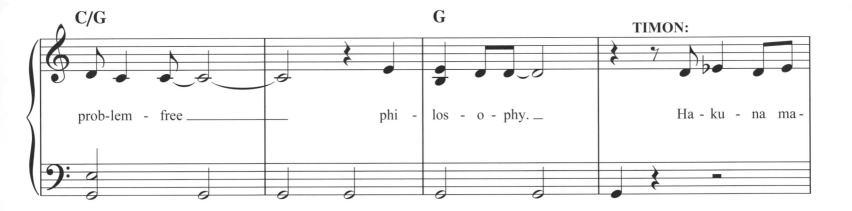

prob-lem - free _____ phi - los - o - phy. _ **TIMON:** Ha - ku - na ma-

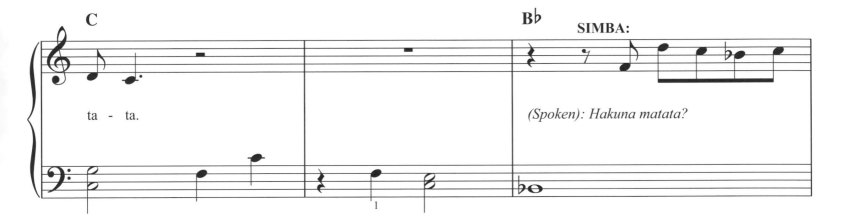

ta - ta. *(Spoken): Hakuna matata?* **SIMBA:**

PUMBAA: *Yeah, it's our motto.* **SIMBA:** *What's a motto?* **TIMON:** *Nothin'! What's-a-motto with you?*

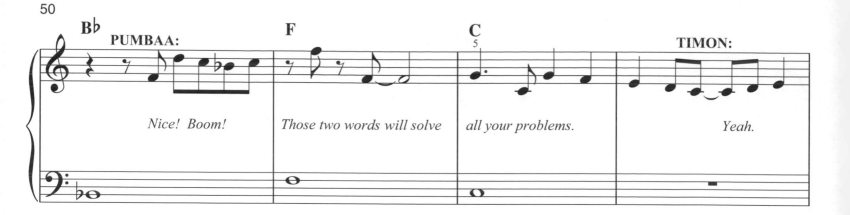

PUMBAA:

Nice! Boom! | Those two words will solve | all your problems. | **TIMON:** Yeah.

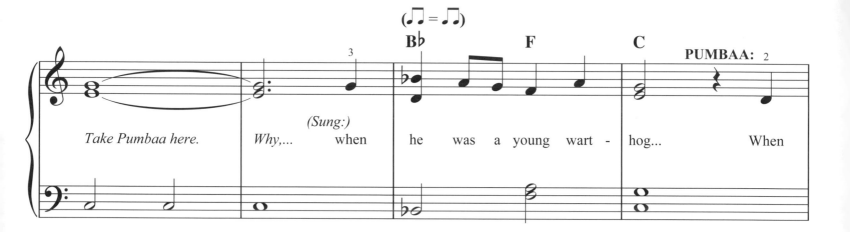

Take Pumbaa here. | Why,... *(Sung:)* when | he was a young wart - hog... | **PUMBAA:** When

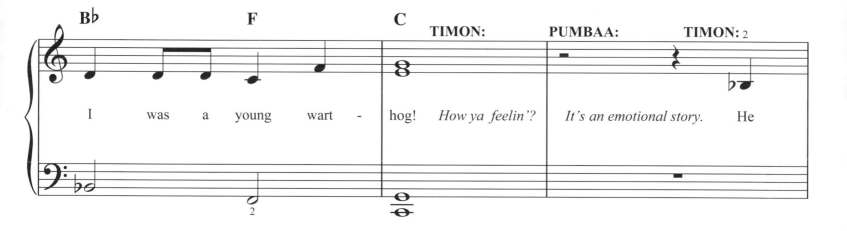

I was a young wart - hog! | **TIMON:** *How ya feelin'?* | **PUMBAA:** *It's an emotional story.* | **TIMON:** He

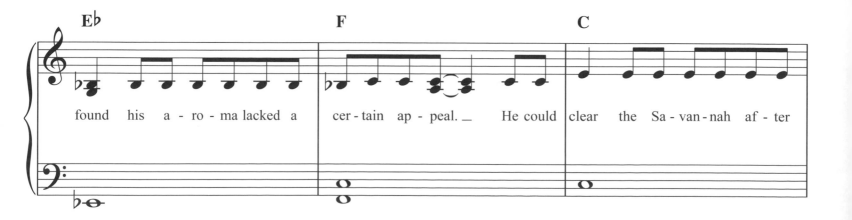

found his a - ro - ma lacked a | cer - tain ap - peal. __ He could | clear the Sa - van - nah af - ter

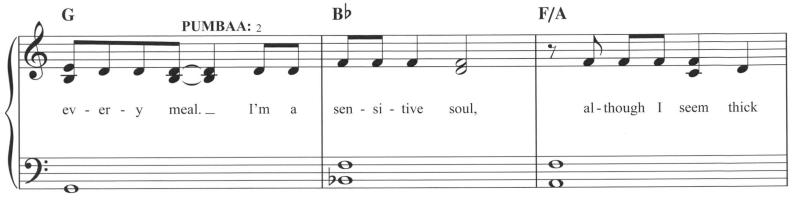

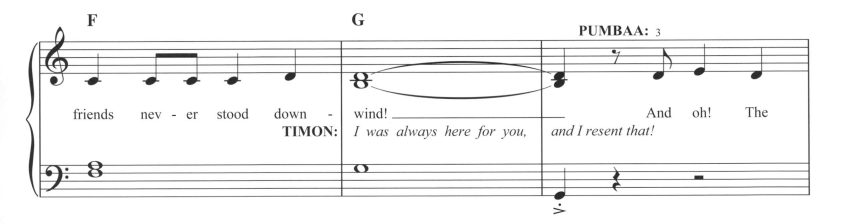

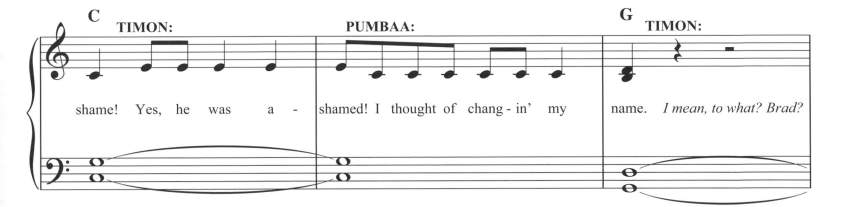

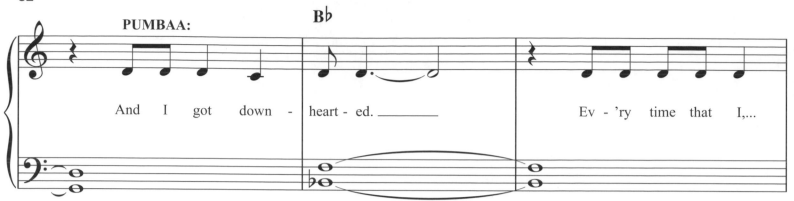

PUMBAA:

And I got down - heart - ed. _____ Ev - 'ry time that I,...

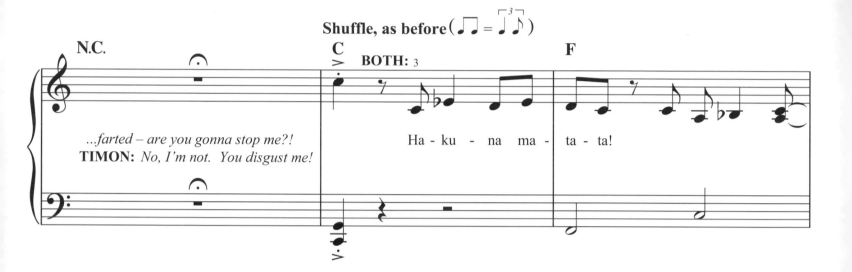

Shuffle, as before (♩♩ = ♩♪)

...*farted – are you gonna stop me?!*
TIMON: *No, I'm not. You disgust me!*

Ha - ku - na ma - ta - ta!

What a won-der - ful phrase. Ha - ku - na ma - ta - ta

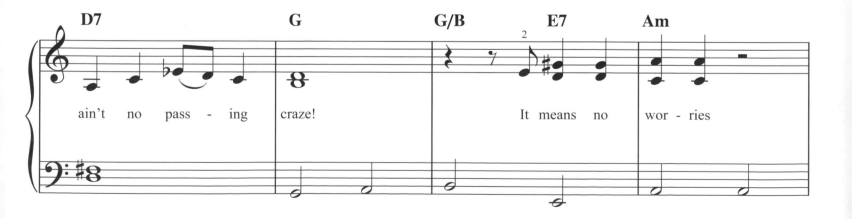

ain't no pass - ing craze! It means no wor - ries

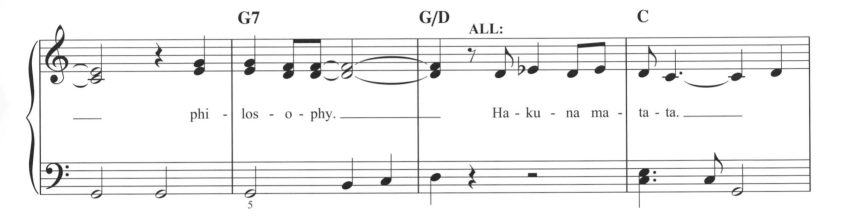

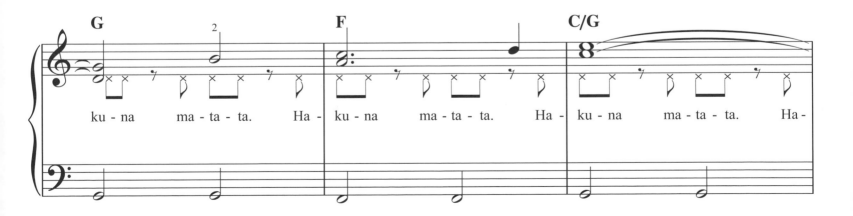

54

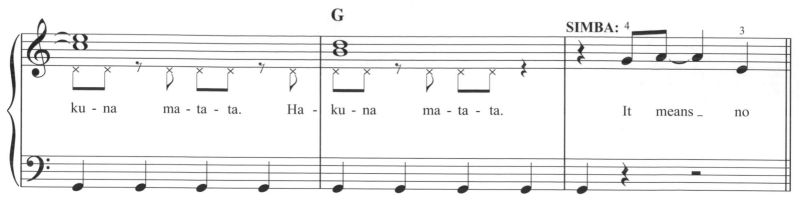

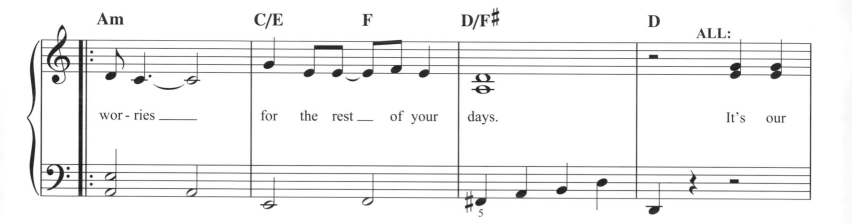

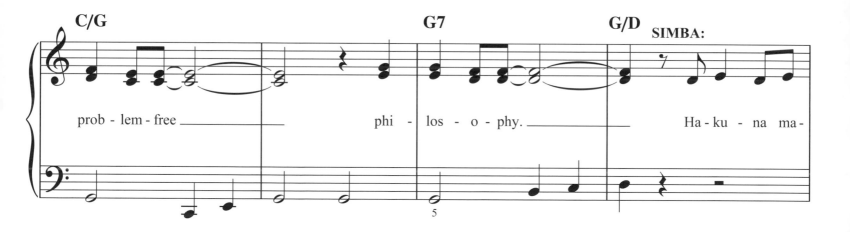

ta - ta, _____ oh, _____ ho, ah. _____

It means _ no

2.

ta - ta.

SIMBA IS ALIVE!

Composed by
HANS ZIMMER

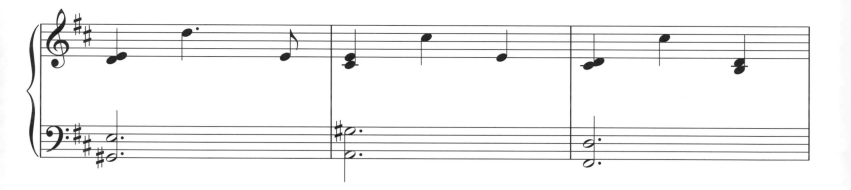

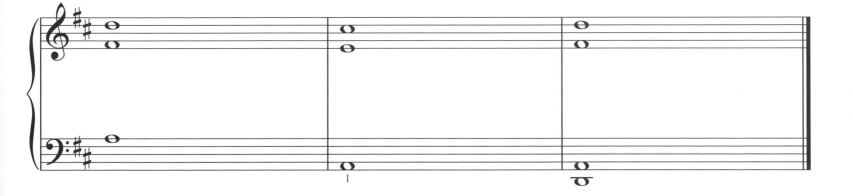

THE LION SLEEPS TONIGHT

New Lyrics and Revised Music by GEORGE DAVID WEISS,
HUGO PERETTI and LUIGI CREATORE

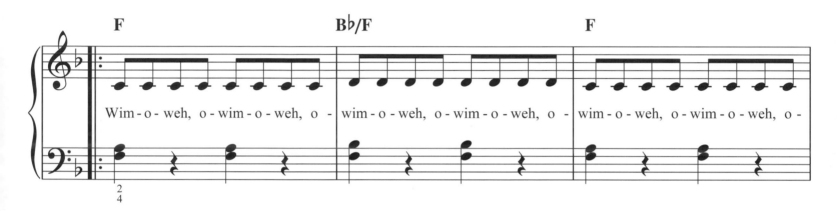

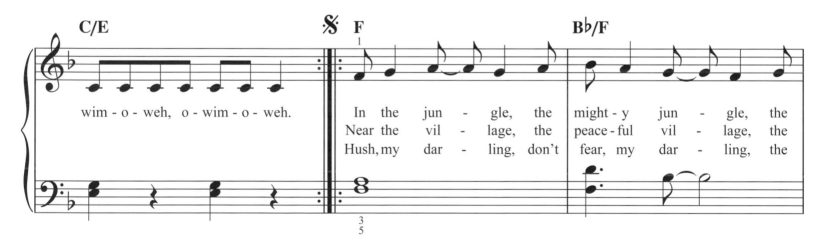

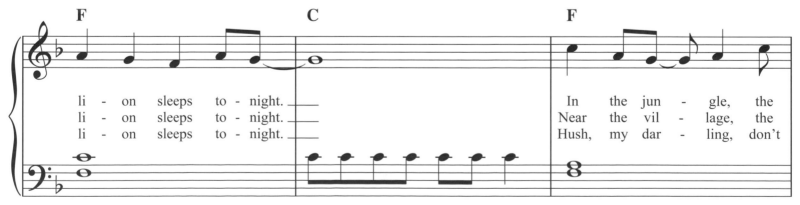

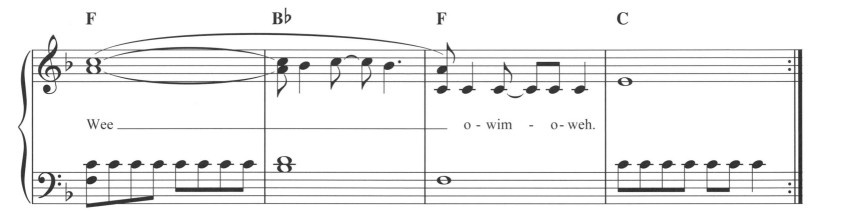

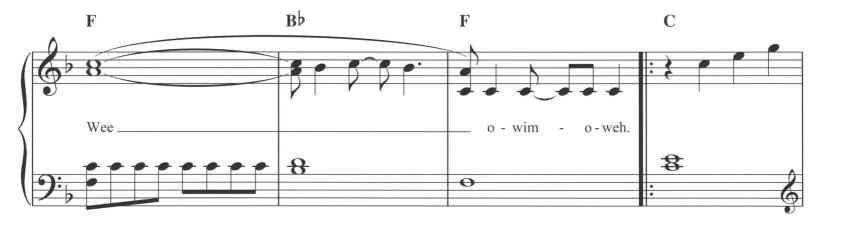

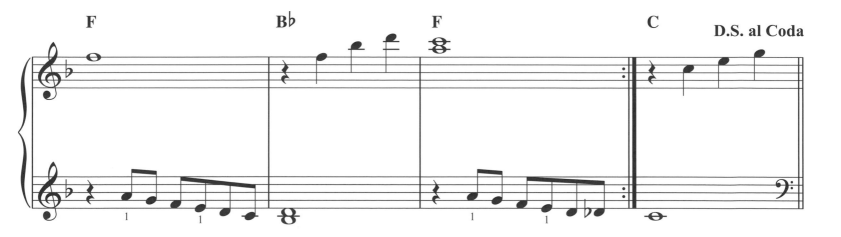

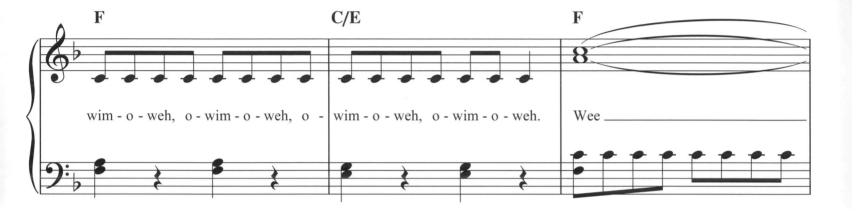

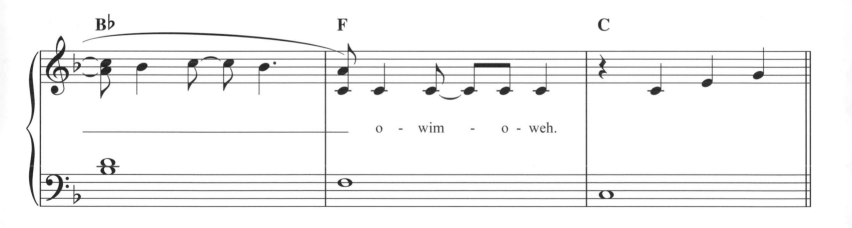

CAN YOU FEEL THE LOVE TONIGHT

Music by ELTON JOHN
Lyrics by TIM RICE

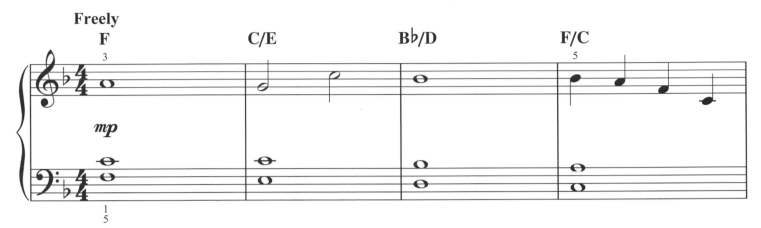

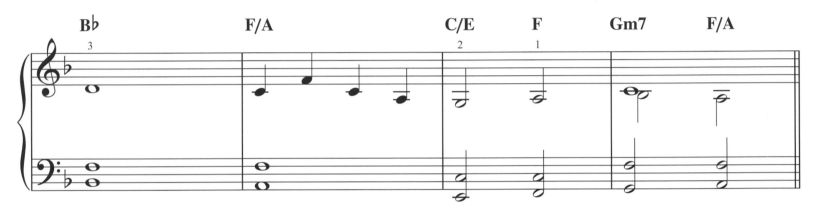

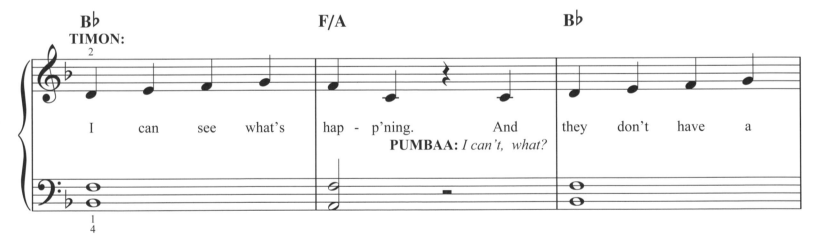

I can see what's hap-p'ning. And they don't have a
PUMBAA: *I can't, what?*

clue. They'll fall in love and here's the bot-tom line: Our
Who's they?

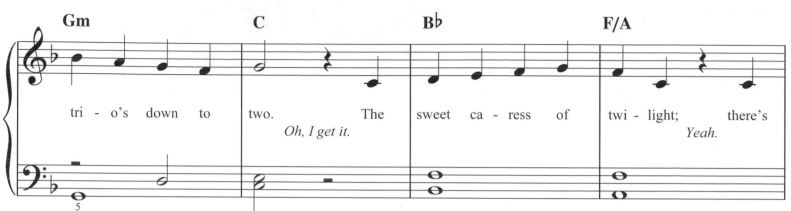

Gm · C · B♭ · F/A

tri - o's down to two. The sweet ca - ress of twi - light; there's
Oh, I get it. *Yeah.*

B♭ · F/A · B♭ · Dm7 · Am/C

mag - ic ev - 'ry - where. And with all this ro - man - tic
It's everywhere. *rall.*

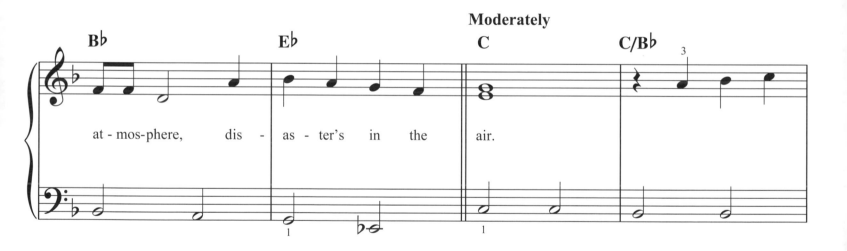

Moderately

B♭ · E♭ · C · C/B♭

at - mos-phere, dis - as - ter's in the air.

Am · C/G · F · C/E · Dm

NALA & SIMBA:

cresc. Can you feel ___ the love ___

mf

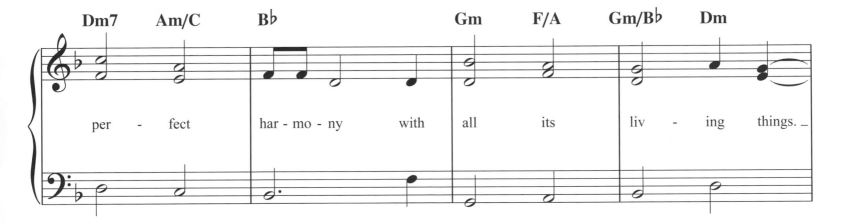

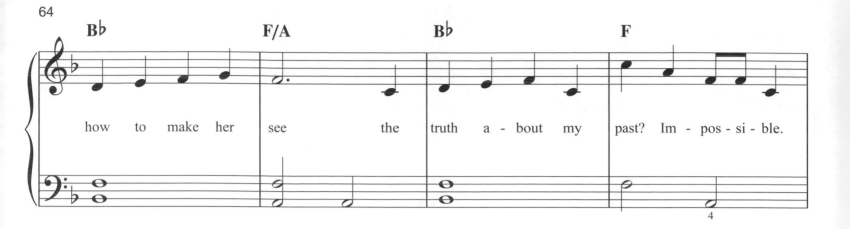

how to make her see the truth a - bout my past? Im - pos - si - ble.

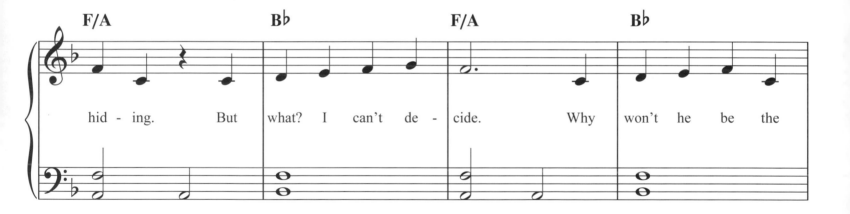

She'd turn a - way from me. _____ **NALA:** He's hold - ing back, he's

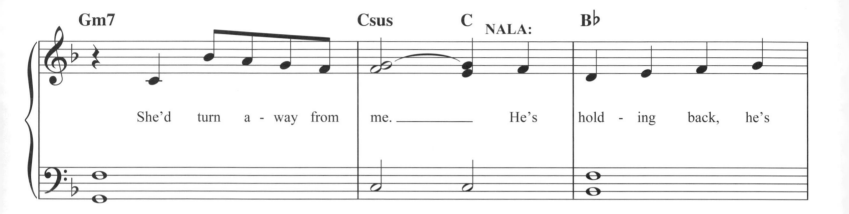

hid - ing. But what? I can't de - cide. Why won't he be the

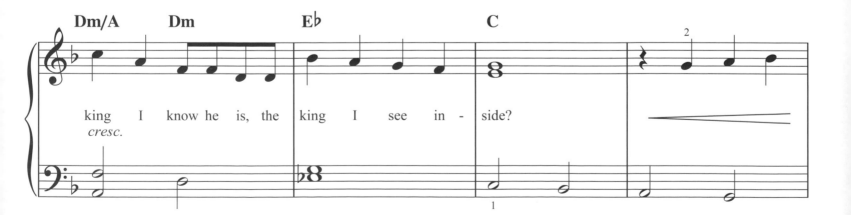

king I know he is, the king I see in - side?

cresc.

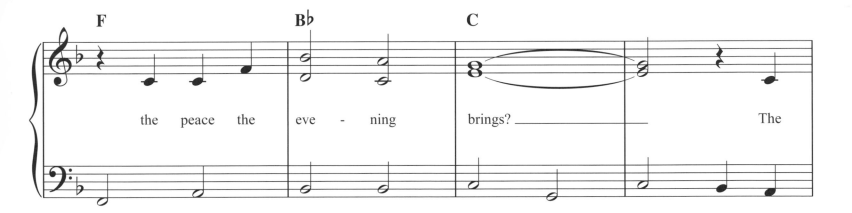

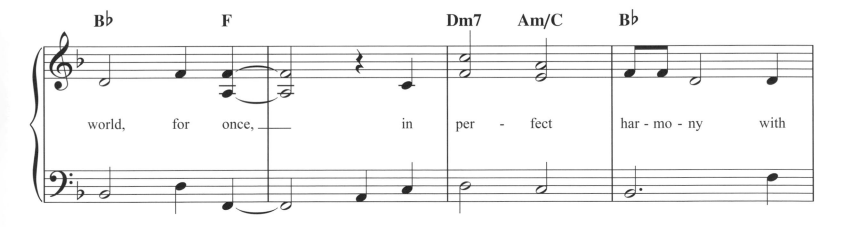

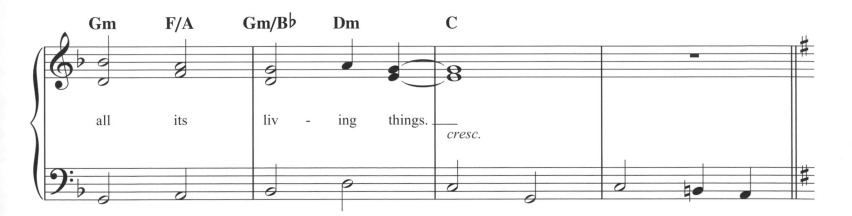

66

Can you feel _____ the love _____ to - night?

f

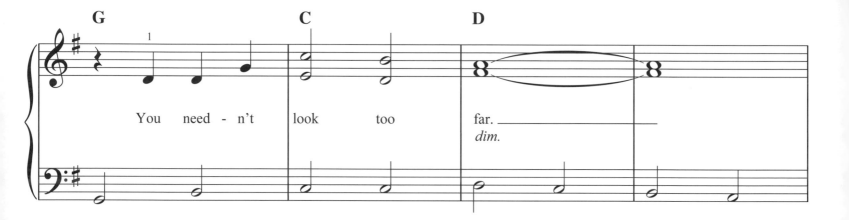

You need - n't look too far. _____

dim.

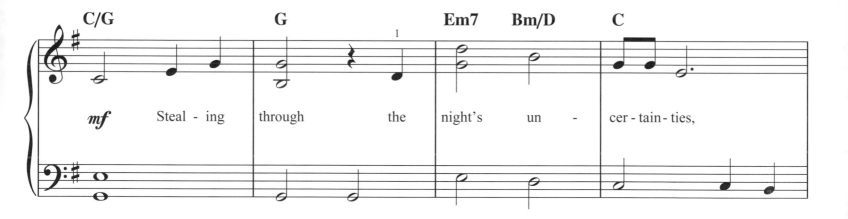

Steal - ing through the night's un - cer - tain - ties,

mf

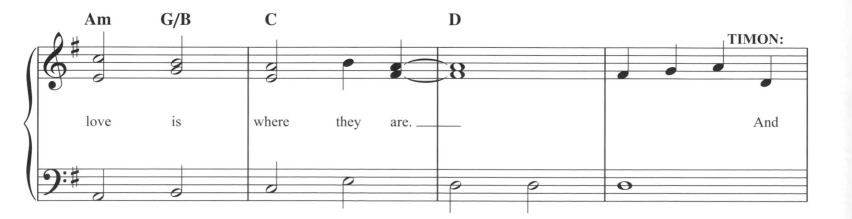

love is where they are. _____

TIMON:

And

67

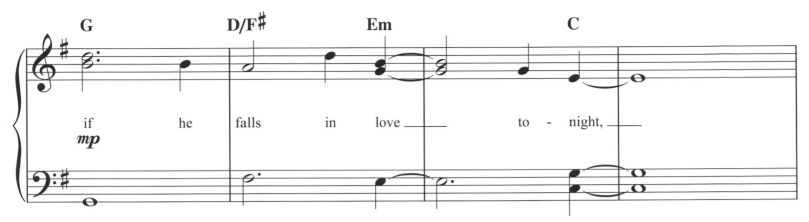

if he falls in love _____ to - night, _____

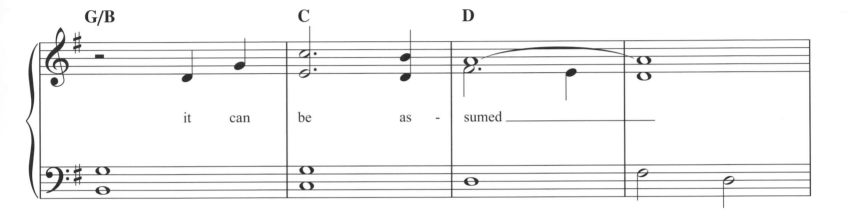

it can be as - sumed _____

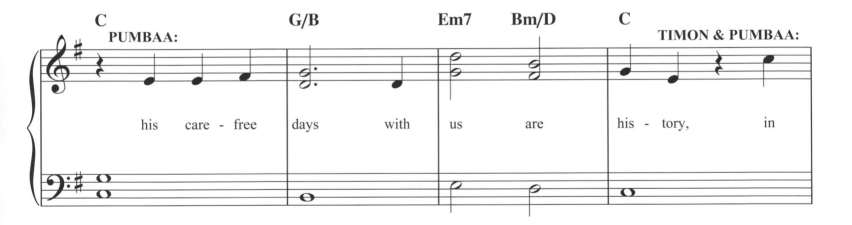

PUMBAA:

his care - free days with us are

TIMON & PUMBAA:

his - tory, in

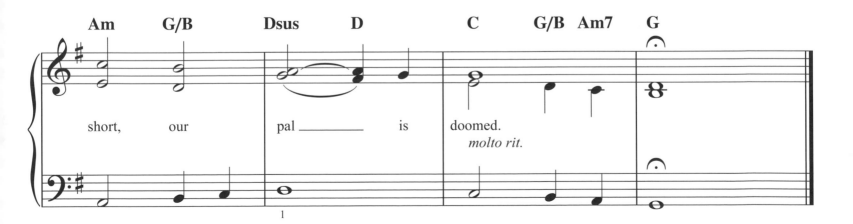

short, our pal _____ is doomed.

molto rit.

SPIRIT

Words and Music by TIMOTHY McKENZIE,
ILYA SALMANZADEH and BEYONCÉ

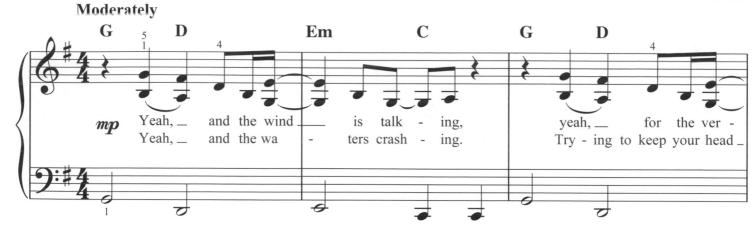

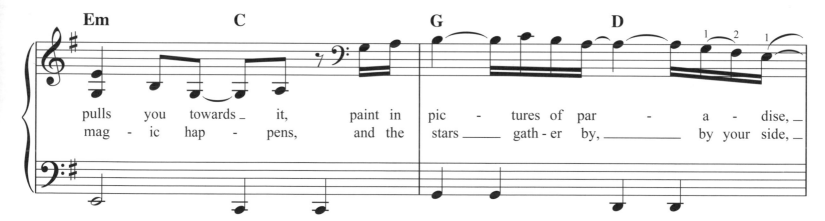

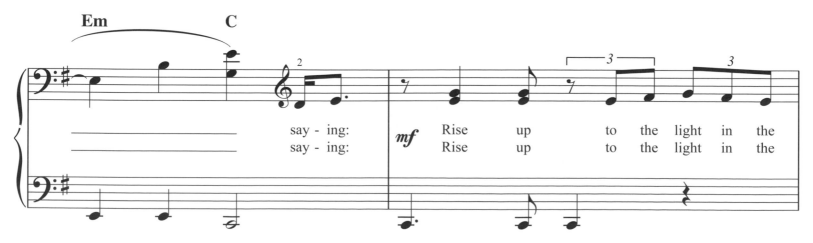

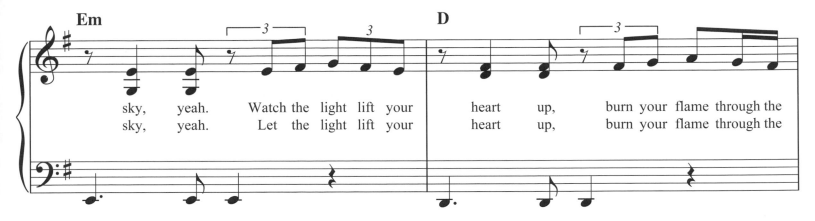

sky, yeah. Watch the light lift your heart up, burn your flame through the
sky, yeah. Let the light lift your heart up, burn your flame through the

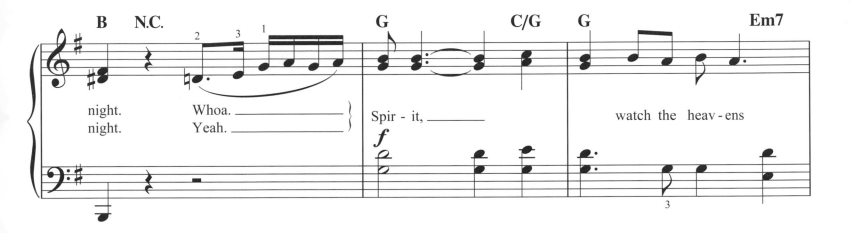

night. Whoa.⸻ Spir - it,⸻ watch the heav - ens
night. Yeah.⸻

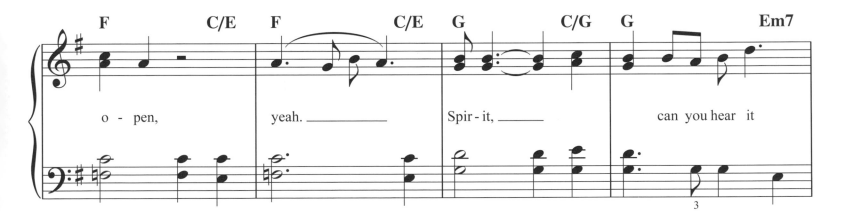

o - pen, yeah.⸻ Spir - it,⸻ can you hear it

call - ing? Yeah.⸻

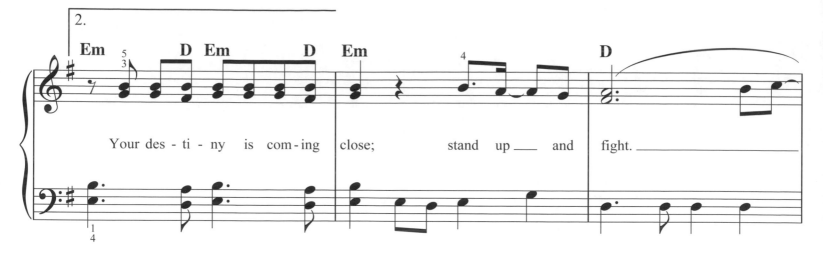

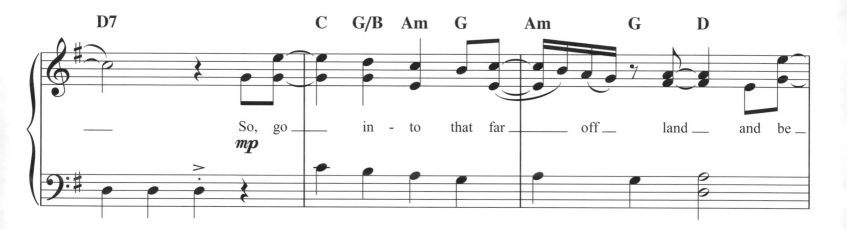

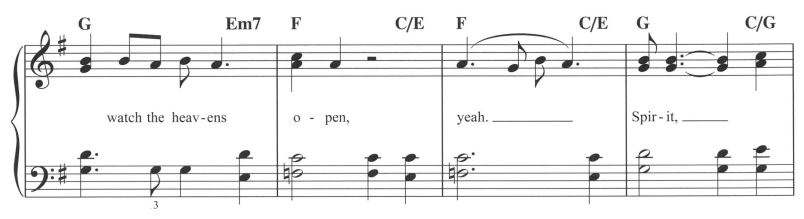

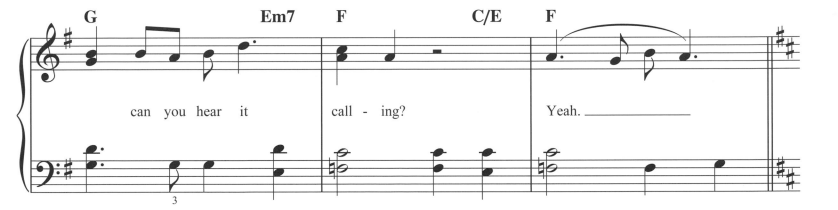

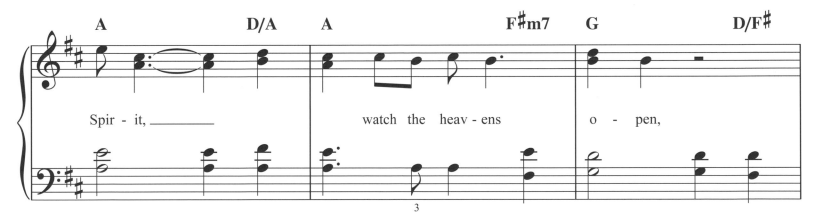

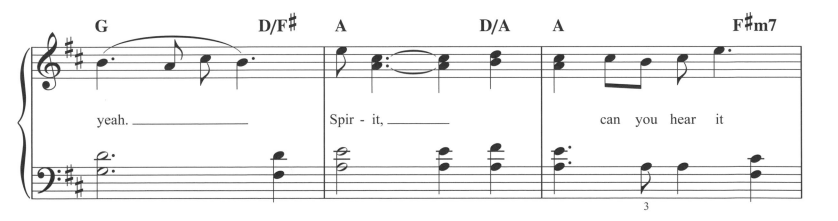

call - ing? Yeah. _____ Your des - ti - ny is com - ing

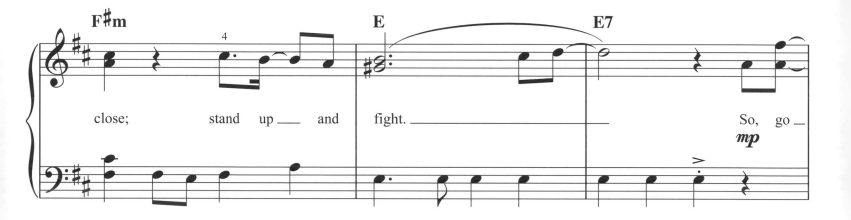

close; stand up _____ and fight. _____ So, go _____

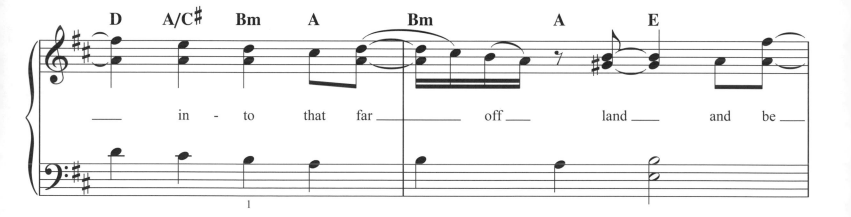

_____ in - to that far _____ off _____ land _____ and be _____

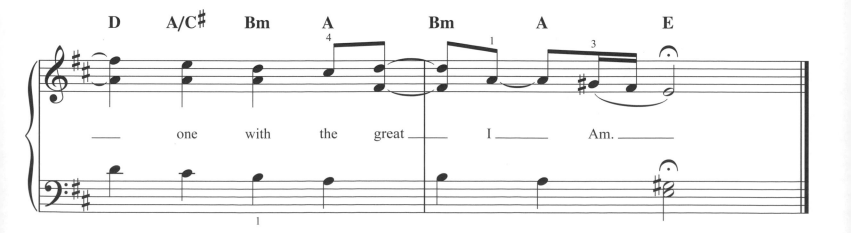

_____ one with the great _____ I _____ Am. _____

BATTLE FOR PRIDE ROCK

Composed by
HANS ZIMMER

Moderately slow, expressively

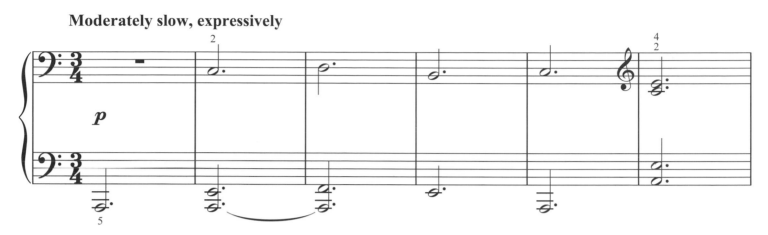

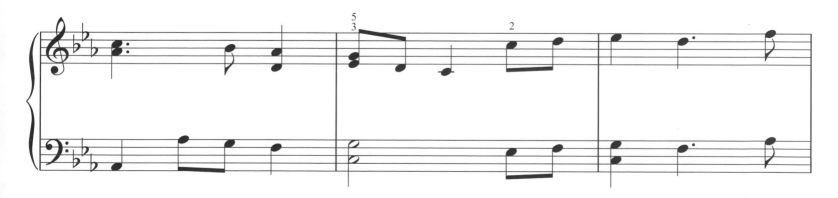

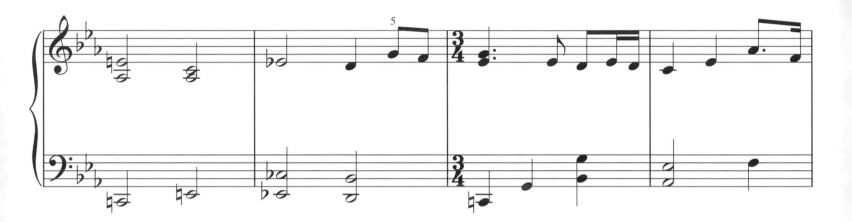

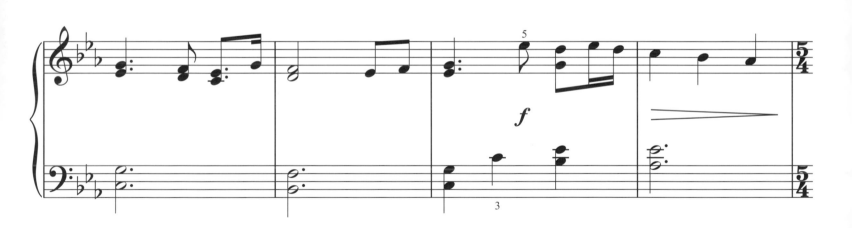

Moderately

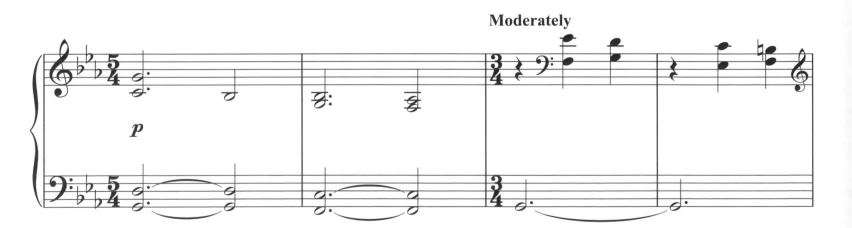

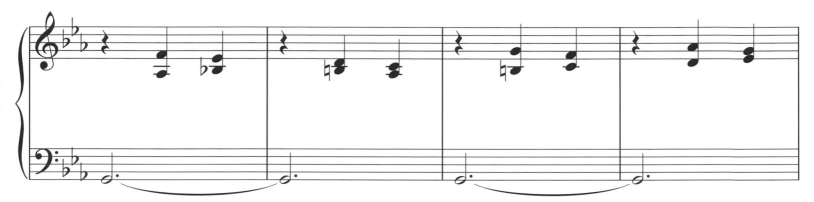

Slowly, steadily

Moderately slow

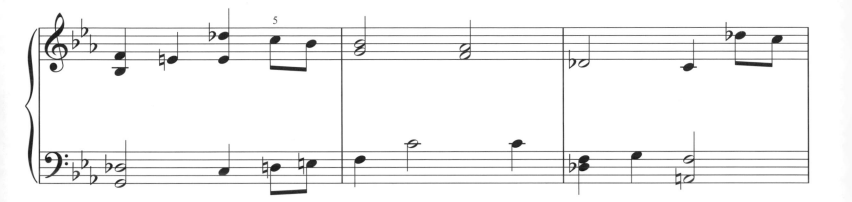

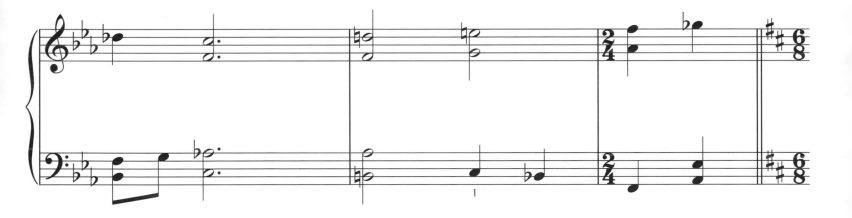

Quickly, in 2

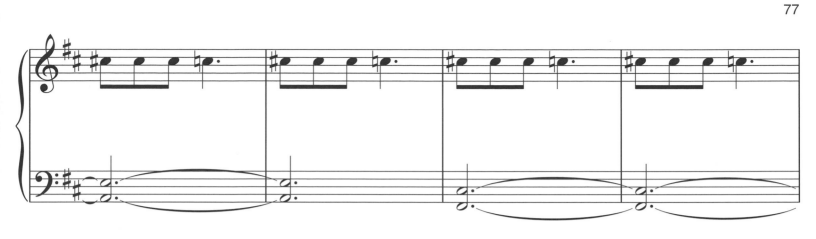

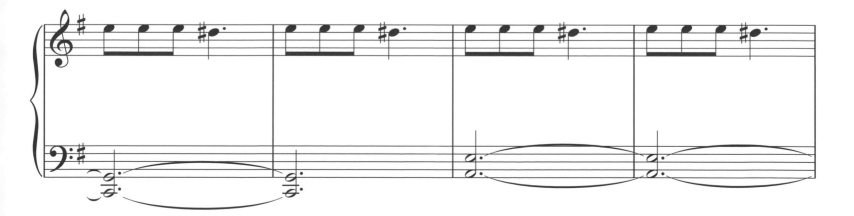

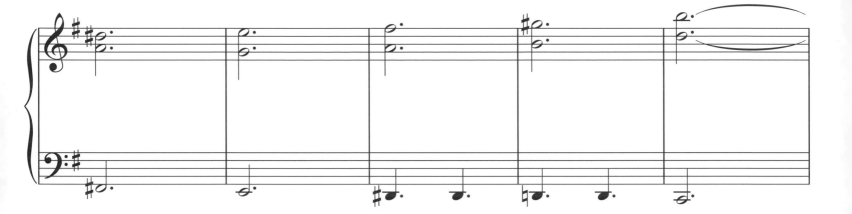

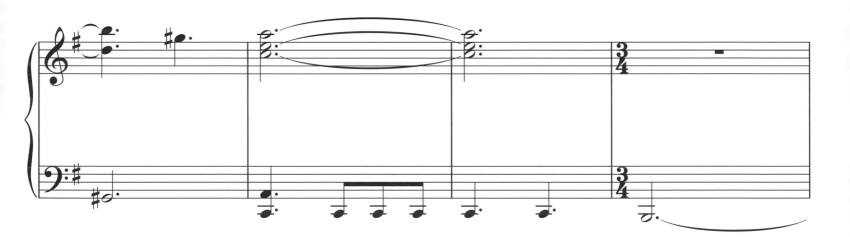

Moderately slow

mf

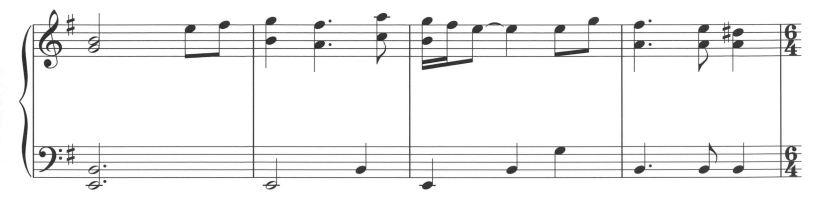

Majestically

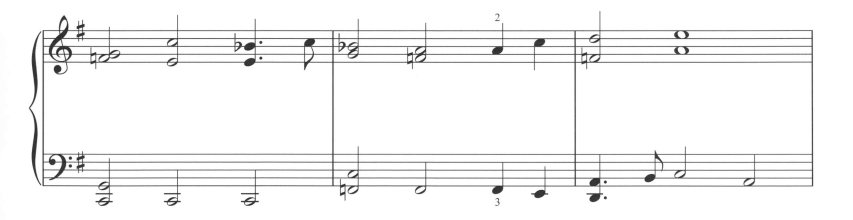

REMEMBER

Composed by
HANS ZIMMER
"Circle of Life" Music by ELTON JOHN,
Lyrics by TIM RICE

Slowly

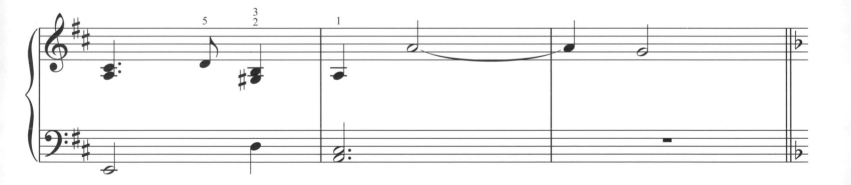

Slightly faster

Quickly, in 1

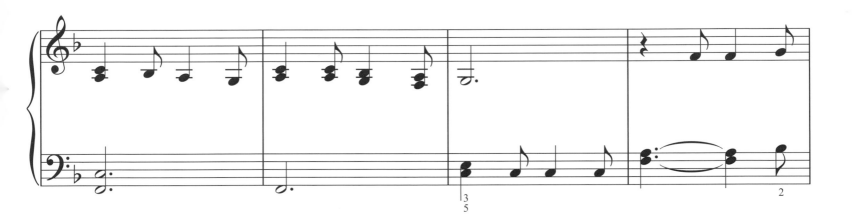

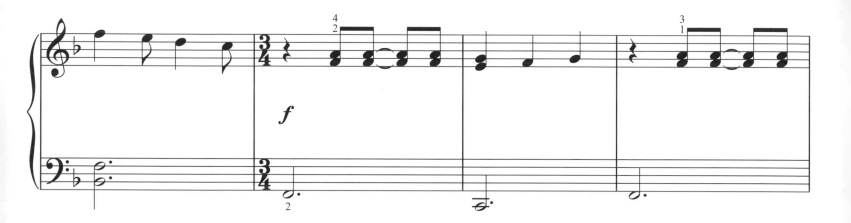

Moderately

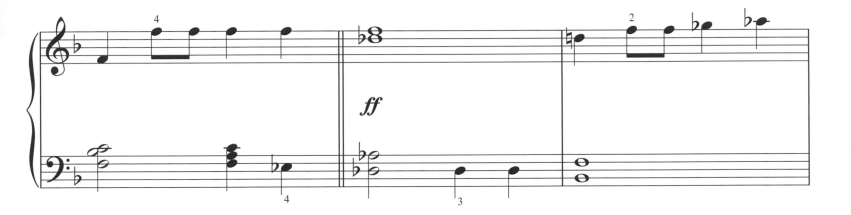

NEVER TOO LATE

Music by ELTON JOHN
Lyrics by TIM RICE

Moderately fast

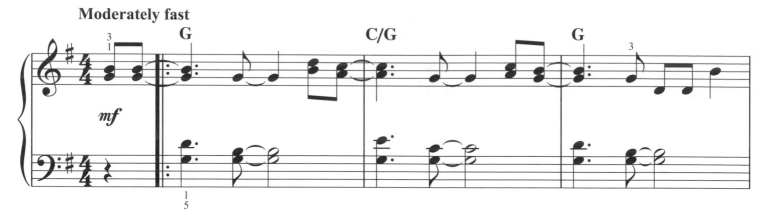

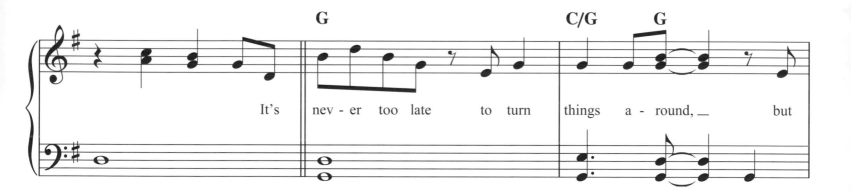

It's nev-er too late to turn things a-round, __ but

come and un-rav - el the path __ to con-found. __ The doubt-ers and los - ers, that line __

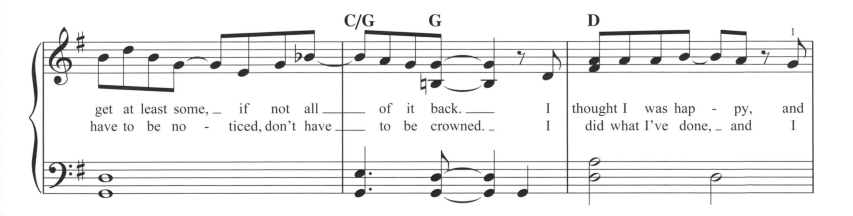

some-times I was, _ but
don't try to hide. _ I

sad-ness is just ____ as im-por - tant be-cause, got to car -
lost man - y things, _ but nev - er my pride. It's nev -

- ry the weight _ and hope ____ it's nev - er too late. ____
- er too late, ____ I know, ____ it's nev - er too late. ____

Nev-er too late to fight the fight.

Nev-er too late to cheat the night.

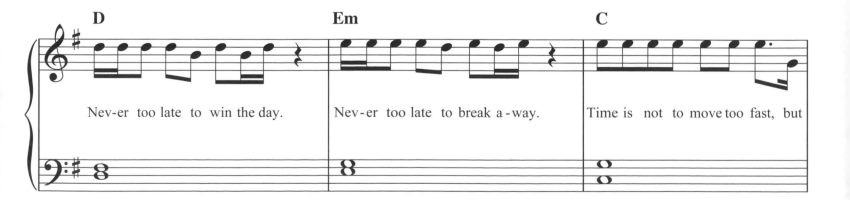

Nev-er too late to win the day.

Nev-er too late to break a-way.

Time is not to move too fast, but

time is not my friend. I'm a long way from the start, but fur-ther from the end.

Oh, _____ it's nev-er too late. _____ It's

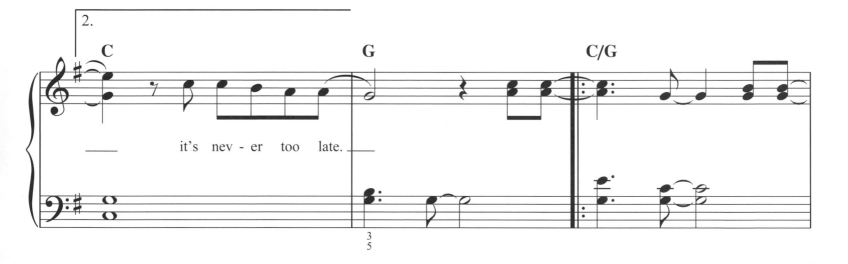

_____ it's nev-er too late. _____

I used to say, "I don't have time, I'm

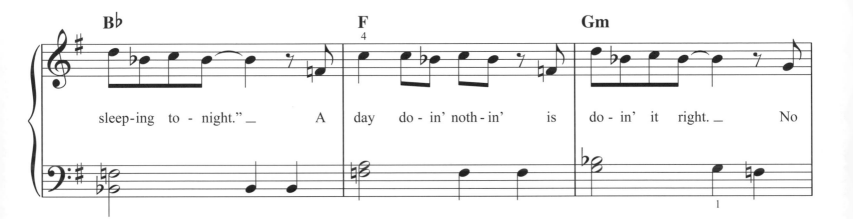

sleep-ing to - night." _ A day do - in' noth-in' is do - in' it right. _ No

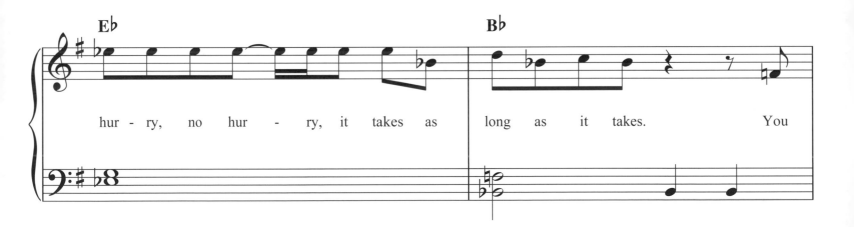

hur - ry, no hur - ry, it takes as long as it takes. You

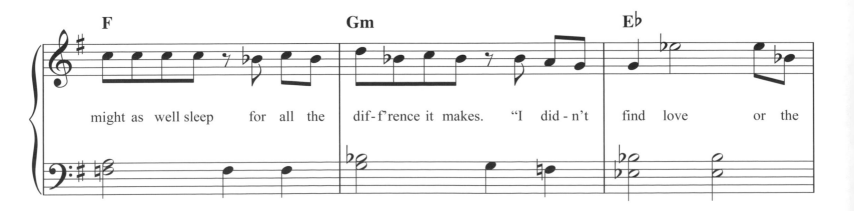

might as well sleep for all the dif-f'rence it makes. "I did - n't find love or the

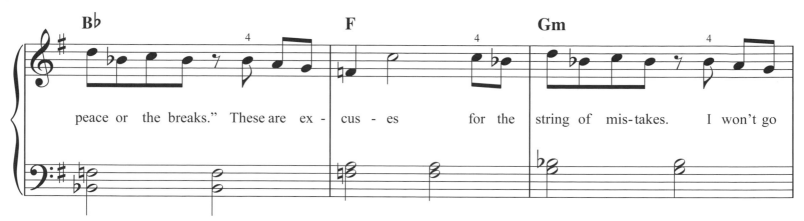

peace or the breaks." These are ex - cus - es   for the   string of mis-takes.   I won't go

back   there.   Not   go - ing   back   there.

Nev-er too late   to fight the fight.

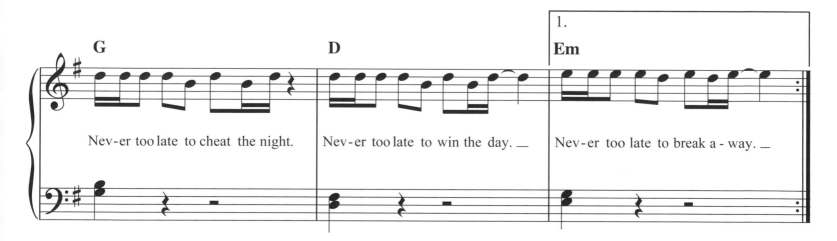

Nev-er too late to cheat the night.   Nev-er too late to win the day. __   Nev-er too late to break a - way. __

92

It's nev - er too late.

It's nev - er too late.   It's nev - er too late.

C/G   **G**

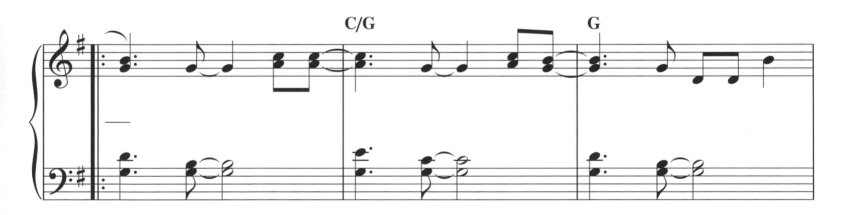

1., 2.   **3.**

HE LIVES IN YOU

Music and Lyrics by MARK MANCINA,
JAY RIFKIN and LEBOHANG MORAKE

Moderately fast

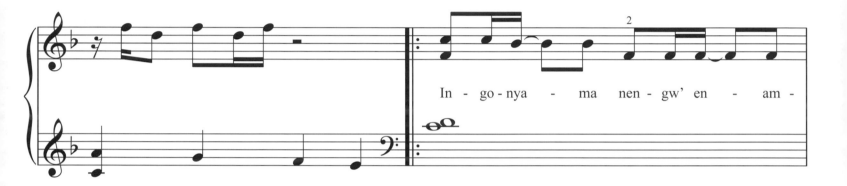

In - go - nya - ma nen - gw' en - am -

ba - la.   In - go - nya - ma nen - gw' en - am -

1.
ba - la.

2.
ba - la.   U - bu - su -

ku

no mo - ya wo - bo - mi

bu - ya-ku-bi - za. _____

Ma - me - la. _____

_____

Ne - zwi.

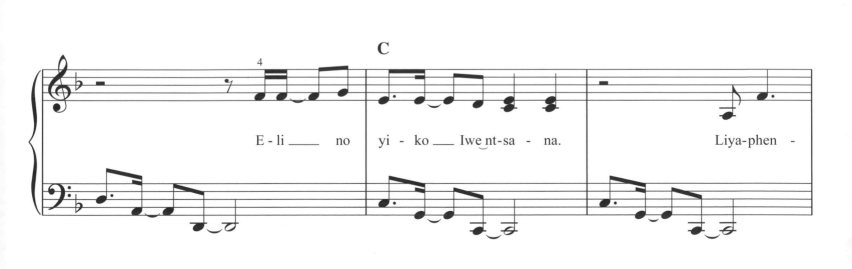

E - li _____ no yi - ko _____ Iwe nt-sa - na.

Liya-phen -

du - la, ___ whoa, ___ ma - me - la.

U - bu - kho - si bo kho - kho. ___

Yi - ma. ___ A - ku -

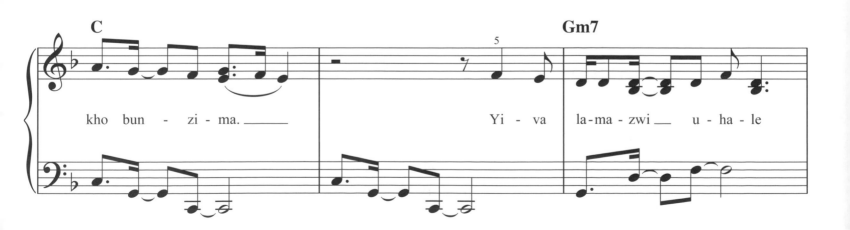

kho bun - zi - ma. ___ Yi - va la - ma - zwi ___ u - ha - le

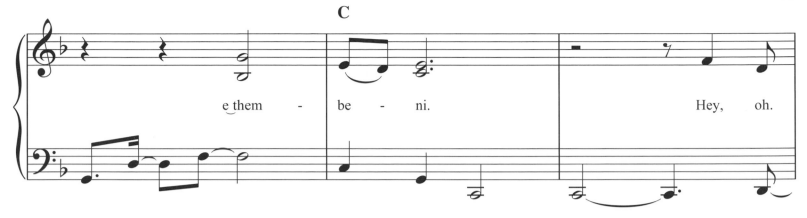

e them - be - ni. Hey, oh.

He - la, yi - ba - ne - them - ba. He - la, yi - ba - ne - them - ba.

He - la, yi - ba - ne - them - ba. U - phi - la

ku - we. U - phi - la ___ na - kum.

U – hla – l'e – jon – gi - le.   Yonk - in -to en siyi bo -

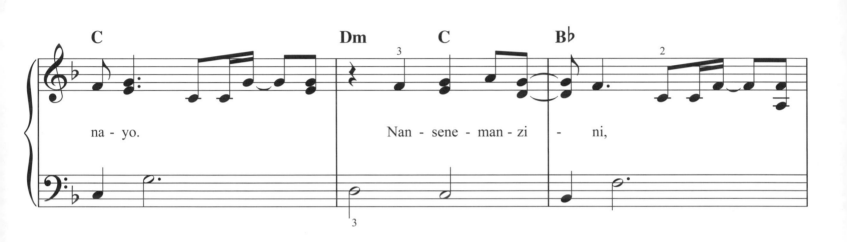

na - yo.   Nan - sene - man - zi - ni,

na – sen – ya – ni – swe – ni.   Na - se mfa-ne - ki - swe -

– ni wa - kho.   U - phi - la ____ ku - we.

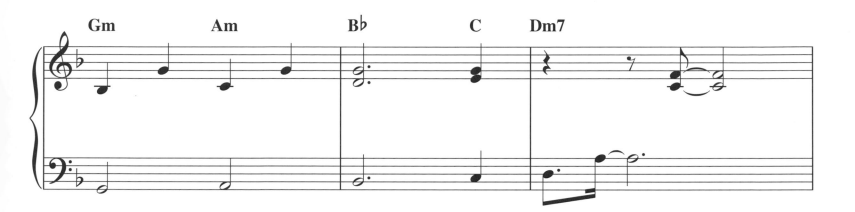

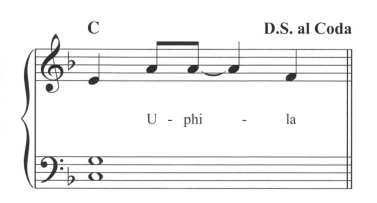

U - phi - la

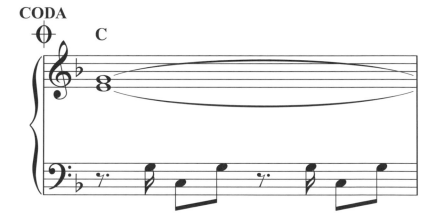

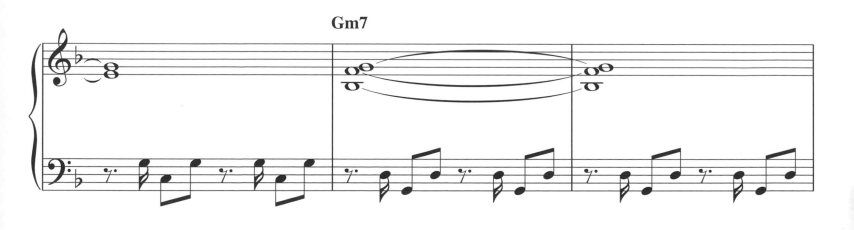

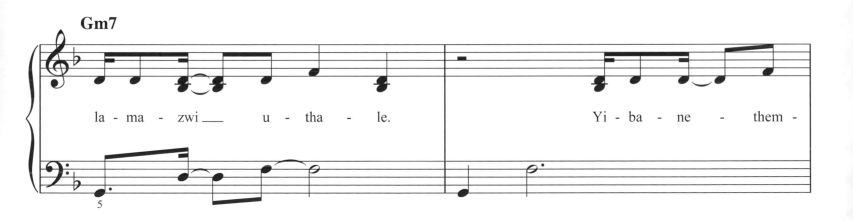

U - phi - la ____ na - kum. U - hla - l'e - jon - gi -

- le. Yonk - in - to en si yi bo -

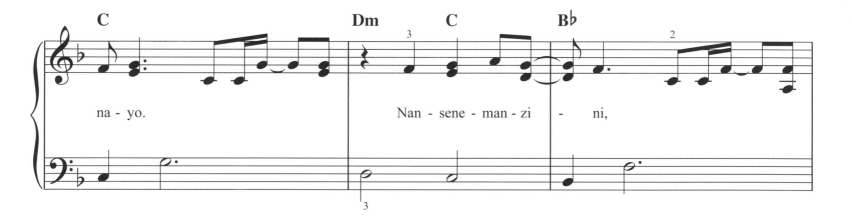

na - yo. Nan - sene - man - zi - ni,

na - sen - ya - ni - swe - ni. Na - se mfa - ne - ki - swe -

English Translation

Here is a lion and a striped tiger.
Night and the spirit of life, calling. Listen.
And a voice, with the fear of a child, answers. Listen.
Throne of the ancestors.
Wait. There's no mountain too great.
Hear these words and have faith. Have faith.
Hey, listen.
He lives in you. He lives in me.
He watches over everything we see.
Into the water, into the truth,
In your reflection, he lives in you.
He lives in you.
Wait. There's no mountain too great.
Hear these words and have faith. Have faith.
He lives in you. He lives in me.
He watches over everything we see.
Into the water, into the truth,
In your reflection, he lives in you.
He lives in you.